UNLOCK THE POWER OF UNDERSTANDING

Ignite Your Path to Transformation

AMOS ETIMIGHAN

Contents

INTRODUCTION

Welcome to the extraordinary journey of unlocking the power of understanding—a journey that holds the key to personal growth, profound connections, and transformative change.

In a world filled with complexities and diverse perspectives, understanding serves as a guiding light that illuminates our path, enabling us to navigate the intricacies of human interactions and discover the transformative potential that lies within.

"Unlocking the Power of Understanding: Ignite Your Path to Transformation" is an invitation to embark on this transformative journey—a journey that transcends the boundaries of knowledge and comprehension, empowering us to cultivate empathy, broaden our perspectives, and foster genuine connections with others. In this comprehensive guide, we will delve into the depths of understanding, unraveling its intricacies, and equipping you with the tools and insights needed to harness its transformative power in your own life.

This book serves as a compass, pointing you towards a transformative shift in how you perceive and engage with the world. It is a roadmap that navigates through the realms of empathy, active listening, curiosity, and open-mindedness, guiding you to unlock the door to understanding and ignite the flames of personal and collective transformation.

Through captivating narratives, thought-provoking exercises, and expert guidance, "Unlocking the Power of Understanding" will empower you to transcend the superficial and tap into the essence of understanding. You will learn to embrace empathy as a powerful force that bridges divides and fosters connection, to actively listen and uncover the deeper meanings behind words, and to cultivate a curious mindset that propels you towards growth and insight.

As you embark on this transformative journey, you will witness the profound impact of understanding on your personal relationships, professional endeavors, and societal contributions. You will discover how understanding empowers you to resolve conflicts, foster collaboration, and become an agent of positive change in a world hungry for compassion and connection.

Embrace this invitation to unlock the power of understanding, and embark on a journey that will ignite your path to transformation. Let this book serve as a guiding companion, supporting you as you navigate the intricacies of understanding, and empowering you to create a life filled with empathy, growth, and profound human connections.

In a fast-paced, interconnected world, the power of understanding has become an indispensable force that can elevate our lives and reshape our collective future. It is the key that unlocks the doors to empathy, insight, and meaningful connections. Imagine a world where understanding flourishes, where conflicts are resolved with compassion, and where individuals thrive in harmony. This book, "Unlock the Power of Understanding: Ignite Your Path to Transformation," is your comprehensive guide to harnessing this extraordinary power within yourself and making a lasting impact on the world around you.

Are you ready to set sail on this voyage of transformation? Open the door, turn the page, and let the power of understanding guide you towards a future filled with empathy, insight, and boundless possibilities.

CHAPTER ONE

THE ESSENCE OF UNDERSTANDING

The Essence of Understanding: Unveiling the Key to Human Connection

In the intricate tapestry of human existence, understanding stands as an invaluable thread that weaves together the fabric of our relationships, societies, and collective progress. It is the gateway to empathy, insight, and harmonious coexistence. Understanding, at its core, transcends mere comprehension; it is a profound appreciation and acknowledgement of the multifaceted complexities that shape our shared human experience. This essay delves into the essence of understanding, exploring its significance, dimensions, and transformative potential in fostering genuine connections and enriching our lives.

Understanding encompasses a multitude of dimensions, each contributing to its rich tapestry. First and foremost, understanding involves empathy—the ability to step into another person's shoes, to feel what they feel, and to genuinely connect with their emotions. Empathy forms the bedrock of understanding, allowing us to transcend our own perspectives and engage with the world through a lens of compassion.

Beyond empathy, understanding requires active listening—the art of not just hearing words but truly comprehending their deeper meanings. It is about creating space for others to express themselves authentically, without judgment or interruption. Active listening enables us to grasp the subtleties beneath the surface, uncovering hidden layers of meaning and paving the way for profound understanding.

Curiosity serves as another pillar of understanding. By nurturing a genuine desire to learn and explore, we open ourselves to the vast array of knowledge, experiences, and perspectives that exist in the world. Curiosity drives us to question assumptions, challenge preconceived notions, and embark on a lifelong journey of discovery. It fuels intellectual growth and broadens our understanding of the complexities that shape our shared reality.

Effective communication is intrinsically linked to understanding. It involves not only articulating our thoughts and feelings clearly but also interpreting and deciphering the messages conveyed by others. Communication bridges the gap between diverse minds, fostering understanding through the exchange of ideas, stories, and experiences. It is the catalyst for building meaningful connections and transcending the barriers that often separate us.

Understanding thrives in an environment of openness and acceptance. It necessitates the willingness to embrace diversity—be it cultural, social, or intellectual. Embracing diversity broadens our horizons, exposing us to a tapestry of perspectives and fostering a richer understanding of the human condition. By appreciating and respecting our differences, we foster a sense of unity that transcends superficial divides.

The transformative power of understanding manifests in various domains of life. In personal relationships, it strengthens the bonds we share with others, nurturing trust, empathy, and emotional intimacy. In professional settings, understanding cultivates collaboration, innovation, and effective teamwork. At a societal level, understanding lays the groundwork for social harmony, justice, and progress.

Understanding, in its essence, is the foundation upon which human connection is built. It is the thread that weaves together the diverse fabric of our world, fostering empathy, insight, and unity. By embracing the dimensions of empathy, active listening, curiosity, effective communication, and acceptance of diversity, we unlock the transformative potential of understanding. It is through understanding that we can bridge divides, dissolve prejudice, and foster a world where compassion, empathy, and genuine human connection thrive.

As we navigate the complexities of life, let us remember that understanding is not a passive state but an active pursuit—a journey that requires continuous growth, introspection, and a genuine willingness to connect. By nurturing the essence of understanding, we hold the power to transform our relationships, communities, and ultimately, the world we inhabit. Let us embark on this journey of understanding, embracing its significance, and sowing the seeds of empathy, compassion, and profound human connection.

UNVEILING THE TRUE NATURE AND SIGNIFICANCE OF UNDERSTANDING

Understanding, though often taken for granted, is a profound and transformative force that shapes our interactions, relationships, and overall human experience. It is the underlying fabric that connects us, enabling empathy, insight, and meaningful connections to flourish. In this essay, we embark on a journey to unveil the true nature and significance of understanding, exploring its multifaceted dimensions and highlighting its transformative power in fostering harmony, growth, and collective progress.

THE MULTIFACETED DIMENSIONS OF UNDERSTANDING: Understanding encompasses a myriad of dimensions, each contributing to its rich and complex nature. At its core, understanding goes beyond the mere act of knowledge acquisition. It involves a deep appreciation of context, nuance, and the underlying motivations that drive human behavior. Understanding requires us to delve beneath the surface, embracing complexity and embracing the intricacies of the human experience.

Empathy serves as a foundational pillar of understanding. It is the ability to genuinely connect with the emotions, thoughts, and experiences of others, transcending our own perspectives. Empathy allows us to see the world through the eyes of another, to share in their joys and sorrows, and to forge authentic connections built on compassion and mutual respect.

Active listening is another vital component of understanding. It entails not just hearing words, but actively engaging with and comprehending the message being conveyed. Active listening creates space for others to express themselves fully, fostering an environment of trust and validation. By truly listening, we gain access to the depth of someone's thoughts and emotions, leading to a deeper understanding of their perspectives.

Curiosity is an inherent characteristic that fuels the quest for understanding. It is the desire to explore, question, and seek knowledge beyond what is immediately apparent. Curiosity encourages us to challenge assumptions, embrace diverse perspectives, and continuously expand our intellectual horizons. By nurturing curiosity, we foster a thirst for understanding that propels us toward growth and personal development.

THE TRANSFORMATIVE POWER OF UNDERSTANDING: Understanding holds immense significance in shaping our personal growth, relationships, and collective well-being. At an individual level, understanding enables us to navigate the complexities of our own emotions, thoughts, and desires. It promotes self-awareness, fostering a deeper understanding of our strengths, weaknesses, and aspirations. Through self-understanding, we can make informed decisions, pursue meaningful goals, and cultivate a sense of fulfillment.

In interpersonal relationships, understanding builds bridges of connection and fosters healthy communication. When we genuinely seek to understand others, conflicts are mitigated, empathy is nurtured, and trust is strengthened. Understanding encourages open dialogue, where diverse perspectives are valued and consensus is reached through mutual understanding and respect.

At a societal level, understanding is an essential catalyst for social cohesion and progress. It paves the way for inclusive communities, where diversity is celebrated and prejudices are dismantled. It serves as a foundation for resolving conflicts, fostering empathy, and building bridges across cultural, ethnic, and social divides. By embracing understanding, societies can work towards collective solutions, address systemic issues, and create a more just and compassionate world.

Understanding, in its true essence, transcends superficial knowledge or passive recognition. It involves empathy, active listening, curiosity, and a genuine desire to connect and comprehend. Its significance lies in its ability to foster empathy, build bridges of connection, and propel personal and collective growth. As individuals, by cultivating understanding, we can forge deeper relationships, embrace diversity, and lead lives imbued with compassion and insight. At a societal level, understanding holds the key to overcoming barriers, resolving conflicts, and shaping a harmonious and progressive world. Let us embrace the true nature and significance of understanding, and harness its transformative power to unlock a brighter future for all.

EXAMINING THE CORE COMPONENTS AND DIMENSIONS OF UNDERSTANDING

Understanding is a complex and multifaceted concept that lies at the heart of our interactions, relationships, and growth as individuals. To truly grasp its essence, we must delve into its core components and dimensions. In this essay, we embark on a journey of exploration, examining the fundamental elements that constitute understanding and unraveling the intricate dimensions that shape its transformative power. By gaining a deeper understanding of understanding itself, we can navigate the intricacies of human connection and foster a world where empathy, insight, and harmonious coexistence thrive.

THE CORE COMPONENTS OF UNDERSTANDING:

COMPREHENSION: At the core of understanding lies comprehension—the ability to grasp information, ideas, or concepts. It involves absorbing knowledge, recognizing patterns, and making sense of the world around us. Comprehension serves as the foundation upon which understanding is built, allowing us to gain insight into the complexities of various subjects and phenomena.

CONTEXTUAL AWARENESS: Understanding extends beyond mere comprehension; it involves contextual awareness. This component requires us to consider the broader context in which information is presented or experiences are shared. It involves recognizing the underlying factors, influences, and circumstances that shape a situation, enabling us to interpret and comprehend it more holistically.

PERSPECTIVE-TAKING: Central to understanding is the capacity for perspective-taking. It involves stepping outside our own viewpoints and immersing ourselves in the perspectives of others. Perspective-taking requires empathy, active listening, and the ability to suspend judgment, allowing us to gain a deeper understanding of different viewpoints, experiences, and emotions.

THE DIMENSIONS OF UNDERSTANDING:

EMOTIONAL UNDERSTANDING: Understanding encompasses not only intellectual comprehension but also emotional understanding. This dimension involves empathizing with and comprehending the emotional states of others. Emotional understanding enables us to connect on a deeper level, recognizing and validating the feelings and experiences of those around us.

SELF-UNDERSTANDING: An essential dimension of understanding is self-understanding. It involves introspection, self-reflection, and gaining insight into our own thoughts, emotions, and motivations. Self-understanding allows us to navigate our own complexities, recognize our strengths and weaknesses, and foster personal growth and self-acceptance.

CULTURAL UNDERSTANDING: Understanding extends to the realm of culture, embracing cultural diversity and recognizing the significance of different cultural norms, values, and practices. Cultural understanding involves appreciating the richness and nuances of various cultures, promoting inclusivity, and bridging gaps that may arise from cultural differences.

CONTEXTUAL UNDERSTANDING: Contextual understanding emphasizes the importance of comprehending situations, events, or information within their specific contexts. It involves recognizing the broader circumstances, histories, and underlying dynamics that shape a given context. Contextual understanding enables us to make informed judgments, interpretations, and decisions.

Understanding, with its core components and dimensions, is a multidimensional concept that encompasses comprehension, context, perspective-taking, emotional understanding, self-understanding, cultural understanding, and contextual understanding. By exploring these components and dimensions, we gain a deeper appreciation for the complexity of understanding itself. Understanding becomes a dynamic process that transcends surface-level knowledge, promoting empathy, insight, and harmonious connections. As we strive to enhance our understanding, let us embrace the diverse dimensions that underpin it, fostering a world where empathy, curiosity, and mutual understanding thrive.

HIGHLIGHTING THE TRANSFORMATIVE POTENTIAL OF CULTIVATING A DEEP UNDERSTANDING

Cultivating a deep understanding is a transformative journey that has the power to enrich our lives, enhance our relationships, and reshape our perspectives. It goes beyond surface-level knowledge, inviting us to delve into the depths of empathy, critical thinking, and open-mindedness. In this essay, we explore the transformative potential that lies within the cultivation of a deep understanding. By embracing this journey, we can unlock new horizons, ignite personal growth, and contribute to positive change in our communities and the world.

EMPATHY AND CONNECTION:

Cultivating a deep understanding fosters empathy—an essential quality that bridges gaps, nurtures compassion, and strengthens human connections. By immersing ourselves in the experiences and emotions of others, we develop a profound sense of empathy, breaking down barriers of judgment and prejudice. This transformative power of empathy enables us to forge authentic connections, build trust, and promote harmonious relationships.

BROADENED PERSPECTIVES:

A deep understanding expands our perspectives and broadens our worldview. It encourages us to question assumptions, challenge biases, and embrace diverse viewpoints. By recognizing the limitations of our own experiences, we open ourselves to a wealth of knowledge and wisdom from others. This transformative process of embracing multiple perspectives enables personal growth, stimulates creativity, and cultivates a spirit of inclusivity and respect.

CONFLICT RESOLUTION AND COLLABORATION:

Cultivating a deep understanding equips us with the tools to navigate conflicts and foster constructive dialogue. By actively listening, seeking common ground, and striving to comprehend the underlying motivations of others, we can bridge divides and find mutually beneficial solutions. This transformative potential of understanding facilitates collaboration, encourages teamwork, and paves the way for collective success.

PERSONAL GROWTH AND SELF-AWARENESS:

A deep understanding of ourselves and others leads to personal growth and self-awareness. By exploring our own thoughts, emotions, and motivations, we gain insight into our strengths, weaknesses, and aspirations. This transformative journey of self-discovery enables us to make conscious choices, align our actions with our values, and pursue a path of personal fulfillment.

SOCIAL IMPACT AND EMPOWERMENT:

Cultivating a deep understanding empowers us to make a positive impact in our communities and beyond. By engaging in social issues, listening to marginalized voices, and understanding systemic challenges, we become advocates for change. This transformative power of understanding enables us to challenge injustice, promote equality, and contribute to a more just and compassionate society.

Cultivating a deep understanding holds transformative potential that extends far beyond individual growth. It allows us to forge meaningful connections, broaden our perspectives, resolve conflicts, and empower ourselves and others. By embracing this transformative journey, we become catalysts for positive change in our communities and the world at large. Let us commit ourselves to the pursuit of understanding, igniting the transformative potential within us and unlocking a future where empathy, collaboration, and mutual respect thrive.

CHAPTER TWO

EMPATHY: THE GATEWAY TO UNDERSTANDING

In a world that often seems divided and disconnected, empathy emerges as the gateway to understanding— the powerful force that transcends barriers, fosters connection, and cultivates a deep appreciation for the experiences and emotions of others. Empathy, in its purest form, serves as a guiding light that illuminates our path towards a more compassionate and understanding society.

Welcome to the captivating exploration of "Empathy: The Gateway to Understanding." This journey invites you to unlock the transformative potential of empathy, enabling you to forge meaningful connections, bridge divides, and ignite a profound understanding of the world and the people within it.

Within the pages of this enlightening guide, we will embark on a transformative quest to unravel the intricacies of empathy. We will explore its essence, discover its profound impact on our lives and relationships, and learn how to harness its power to foster genuine understanding.

Empathy holds the key to unlocking the doors of connection. It empowers us to step into the shoes of others, to truly see and feel the world through their eyes. By cultivating empathy, we embrace a shared humanity that recognizes the beauty and diversity of the human experience.

Throughout this journey, we will delve into the depths of empathy, exploring its various dimensions and honing the skills that enable us to express and receive empathy authentically. From understanding the importance of active listening to cultivating compassion and developing emotional intelligence, we will equip ourselves with the tools needed to navigate the complexities of human connection.

By embracing empathy, we bridge divides and dissolve barriers. We come to recognize that understanding emerges not only from our own perspectives but from the genuine effort to comprehend the experiences, emotions, and challenges faced by others. Through empathy, we cultivate a deep appreciation for the richness of diverse viewpoints, fostering inclusivity and compassion in our personal and professional interactions.

In a world yearning for connection and understanding, the transformative power of empathy becomes an agent of change. It allows us to resolve conflicts, heal wounds, and build bridges across divides. As we develop our capacity for empathy, we become catalysts for positive change, instilling hope, and fostering unity in a world desperately in need of compassion and understanding.

So, join us on this remarkable journey to explore the depths of empathy and unlock the gateway to understanding. Let us embark on this transformative path, knowing that by cultivating empathy within ourselves, we have the power to transform not only our own lives but also the lives of those around us.

Are you ready to open the door to empathy and embark on a journey of deep understanding? Prepare to be inspired, to be moved, and to witness the extraordinary power of empathy as it paves the way towards a more empathetic, connected, and compassionate world.

EXPLORING EMPATHY AS A FOUNDATIONAL PILLAR OF UNDERSTANDING

Empathy, the ability to understand and share the feelings of others, stands as a foundational pillar of understanding. It serves as the bedrock upon which deep connections, harmonious relationships, and profound insights are built. In this exploration, we embark on a journey to understand the vital role of empathy as a catalyst for understanding. By delving into its essence, significance, and transformative power, we gain a deeper appreciation for empathy's profound impact on our lives and the world around us.

UNDERSTANDING EMPATHY

Empathy is a powerful force that allows us to transcend our own perspectives and genuinely connect with the experiences and emotions of others. It is the capacity to step into someone else's shoes, to feel what they feel, and to see the world through their eyes. Empathy enables us to go beyond mere sympathy or pity, offering a profound understanding and validation of others' experiences.

THE ESSENCE OF EMPATHY

At its core, empathy is a recognition of our shared humanity. It acknowledges that despite our differences, we all experience a range of emotions, face challenges, and long for understanding and connection. Empathy nurtures a deep sense of compassion, fostering a willingness to listen, understand, and support others on their unique journeys.

EMPATHY AS A BRIDGE:

Empathy serves as a bridge that spans the gaps between individuals, cultures, and perspectives. It fosters a sense of connection and unity, dissolving barriers of judgment, prejudice, and misunderstanding. By practicing empathy, we create an environment of trust, mutual respect, and open dialogue, where understanding flourishes.

THE TRANSFORMATIVE POWER OF EMPATHY

Empathy holds transformative power, both at an individual and societal level. On a personal level, empathy enhances our relationships and emotional well-being. It allows us to build deep connections, resolve conflicts with compassion, and provide support and comfort to others in times of need. Through empathy, we cultivate emotional intelligence, self-awareness, and a profound understanding of ourselves and those around us.

At a societal level, empathy has the potential to foster positive change and social progress. By embracing empathy, we can address systemic issues, bridge social divides, and cultivate a more inclusive and compassionate society. Empathy empowers us to stand up against injustice, promote equality, and create a world where understanding and empathy are valued.

CULTIVATING EMPATHY

While empathy is a natural human trait, it can be nurtured and developed through conscious effort. Cultivating empathy involves active listening, suspending judgment, and seeking to understand the perspectives and emotions of others. It requires practicing empathy not only in moments of ease but also in challenging situations, where empathy can lead to healing, resolution, and growth.

Empathy stands as a foundational pillar of understanding, fostering deep connections, compassion, and personal growth. By embracing empathy, we open ourselves to the transformative power of understanding, forging bonds that transcend differences and nurturing a more compassionate and empathetic world. Let us cultivate empathy within ourselves and extend it to others, creating a ripple effect of understanding and empathy that has the potential to transform lives, relationships, and societies.

Developing emotional intelligence to connect with others on a profound level

Nurturing empathy through active listening, perspective-taking, and compassionate communication.

CHAPTER 3:

THE ART OF ACTIVE LISTENING

Active listening is a powerful communication skill that goes beyond simply hearing words. It involves fully engaging with the speaker, understanding their message, and responding in a way that demonstrates empathy and understanding.

It is an art that can enhance relationships, build trust, and foster effective communication in various aspects of life, from personal relationships to professional interactions. Mastering the art of active listening can have a profound impact on both individuals and communities.

Here are some key principles and techniques to help you develop and hone your active listening skills:

GIVE YOUR FULL ATTENTION: Active listening requires your undivided attention. Eliminate distractions, both external and internal, and focus solely on the speaker. Maintain eye contact, nod or provide other non-verbal cues to show your attentiveness.

BE PRESENT IN THE MOMENT: Be fully present in the conversation and avoid allowing your mind to wander. Don't interrupt or formulate responses while the speaker is talking. Instead, stay engaged and listen with genuine curiosity.

SUSPEND JUDGMENT: It's essential to approach the conversation with an open mind, free from preconceived notions or biases. Avoid jumping to conclusions or making assumptions about the speaker or their message. Reserve judgment until you have a complete understanding of their perspective.

DEMONSTRATE EMPATHY: Empathy is a cornerstone of active listening. Try to understand the speaker's emotions and perspectives by putting yourself in their shoes. Show genuine concern and care for their experiences and challenges. Reflect their emotions back to them to let them know you understand and validate their feelings.

Use verbal and non-verbal cues: Encourage the speaker to share more by using verbal cues such as "I see," "Tell me more," or "Go on." Non-verbal cues, like nodding, smiling, or leaning forward, demonstrate your engagement and interest. These cues reassure the speaker that they have your full attention and that you value what they have to say.

PARAPHRASE AND SUMMARIZE: Throughout the conversation, paraphrase and summarize what the speaker has shared to ensure accurate understanding. Repeat key points using your own words, which helps to clarify any confusion and allows the speaker to confirm or provide additional information.

ASK RELEVANT QUESTIONS: Ask open-ended questions that encourage the speaker to delve deeper into their thoughts and feelings. Avoid leading questions or those that can be answered with a simple "yes" or "no."

Thought-provoking questions can help uncover underlying motivations and gain a more comprehensive understanding.

MAINTAIN PATIENCE AND SILENCE: Active listening requires patience. Offer the opportunity for the speaker to fully articulate their thoughts without being interrupted. Embrace moments of silence as they provide an opportunity for reflection and allow the speaker to gather their thoughts.

AVOID OFFERING IMMEDIATE SOLUTIONS: Active listening is not about providing instant advice or solutions. Often, individuals simply need someone to listen and understand their experiences. Focus on being present and supporting the speaker rather than rushing to solve their problems.

PRACTICE ACTIVE LISTENING IN VARIOUS SETTINGS: Active listening can be practiced in all areas of life. Whether you are engaging in personal conversations with loved ones or participating in professional meetings, apply these principles to develop stronger relationships and foster effective communication.

Remember that active listening is a skill that requires practice and continuous improvement. The more you engage in active listening, the better you become at understanding others, building meaningful connections, and creating an environment of trust and respect. By mastering the art of active listening, you open the door to deeper understanding, empathy, and more enriching interactions with those around you.

MASTERING THE ART OF ACTIVE LISTENING TO UNCOVER DEEPER MEANINGS

Mastering the Art of Active Listening to Uncover Deeper Meanings. Active listening is not just about hearing the words someone is saying; it's about going beyond the surface and uncovering the deeper meanings and emotions behind their communication.

It requires a heightened level of attention, empathy, and curiosity. By mastering the art of active listening, you can develop a profound understanding of others, fostering stronger connections and building more meaningful relationships.

Here are some strategies to help you uncover deeper meanings through active listening:

ENGAGE IN REFLECTIVE LISTENING: Reflective listening involves mirroring the speaker's words and emotions back to them. By paraphrasing or summarizing what they've said, you show that you truly understand and are actively processing their message. This technique encourages the speaker to go deeper into their thoughts and feelings, providing you with more profound insights.

PAY ATTENTION TO NON-VERBAL CUES: Communication is not limited to words alone. Non-verbal cues, such as facial expressions, body language, and tone of voice, can reveal a wealth of information about a person's emotions and underlying meanings. Observe these cues closely and consider their implications in conjunction with the speaker's words.

LISTEN FOR THE UNSAID: Often, people may not explicitly express everything they're feeling or thinking. Active listening involves tuning in to the unspoken messages, the pauses, and the nuances in their communication. Be attentive to what is left unsaid and use your intuition to fill in the gaps, allowing for a deeper understanding of their perspective.

SEEK CLARIFICATION AND ASK PROBING QUESTIONS: If something is unclear or if you sense there is more beneath the surface, don't hesitate to seek clarification. Ask open-ended questions that encourage the speaker to elaborate and provide more context. These probing questions can help unveil the underlying motivations, beliefs, or concerns, allowing you to gain a more profound insight into their communication.

EXPLORE EMOTIONS AND FEELINGS: Emotions are powerful indicators of deeper meanings. Actively listen for the emotions conveyed through the speaker's words and tone. Show empathy and ask questions that invite them to delve into their emotional experiences. By understanding the emotional landscape, you can uncover the underlying meanings and motivations behind their communication.

PRACTICE EMPATHY AND PERSPECTIVE-TAKING: Empathy is a fundamental aspect of active listening. Put yourself in the speaker's shoes and try to understand their perspective and experiences. Consider their background, beliefs, and values. This empathetic approach allows you to connect on a deeper level and gain insights that may not be immediately apparent.

BE PATIENT AND COMFORTABLE WITH SILENCE: Sometimes, the most profound meanings emerge during moments of silence. Avoid rushing the conversation or filling the gaps with your own words. Embrace the pauses and allow the speaker to gather their thoughts. Silence can create space for deeper reflection and encourage the speaker to share more meaningful insights.

BE MINDFUL OF YOUR OWN BIASES AND ASSUMPTIONS: Our own biases and assumptions can hinder our ability to uncover deeper meanings. Be aware of your preconceived notions and judgments, and consciously set them aside. Approach the conversation with an open mind, ready to challenge your own beliefs and explore alternative perspectives.

PRACTICE SELF-AWARENESS: Active listening involves being aware of your own reactions, emotions, and thoughts during the conversation. Stay present and avoid getting caught up in your own internal dialogue. By maintaining self-awareness, you can better focus on the speaker's message and uncover the deeper meanings they are trying to convey.

PRACTICE ACTIVE LISTENING REGULARLY: Mastering the art of active listening requires practice. Seek opportunities to engage in meaningful conversations and apply these strategies consistently. As you develop your active listening skills over time, you will become more attuned to the subtleties and uncover deeper meanings effortlessly.

By mastering the art of active listening to uncover deeper meanings, you can build stronger connections, nurture understanding, and develop more meaningful relationships. Remember, it is not only the words that matter but the emotions, nuances, and unspoken messages that hold the key to unlocking profound insights into the human experience.

OVERCOMING BARRIERS TO EFFECTIVE LISTENING AND FOSTERING GENUINE CONNECTIONS

Overcoming Barriers to Effective Listening and Fostering Genuine Connections. Effective listening is crucial for building genuine connections and fostering meaningful relationships.

However, various barriers can hinder our ability to listen attentively and engage fully with others. By identifying and overcoming these barriers, we can improve our listening skills and create deeper connections with those around us.

Here are some common barriers to effective listening and strategies for overcoming them:

DISTRACTIONS: In today's fast-paced world, distractions abound, from technological devices to internal thoughts and concerns. To overcome this barrier, create a conducive listening environment by minimizing external distractions. Put away your phone, find a quiet space, and give your full attention to the speaker. Additionally, practice mindfulness to reduce internal distractions, such as intrusive thoughts or judgments, and focus on being present in the conversation.

PRECONCEIVED NOTIONS AND BIASES: Our preconceived notions and biases can cloud our ability to listen objectively and understand the speaker's perspective.

Overcome this barrier by cultivating self-awareness. Recognize your biases and consciously suspend judgment during conversations. Challenge your assumptions and actively seek to understand different viewpoints. Approach each interaction with an open mind, ready to learn and broaden your understanding.

EMOTIONAL BARRIERS: Strong emotions, such as anger, frustration, or stress, can interfere with effective listening. When we are overwhelmed by our own emotions, it becomes challenging to truly hear and empathize with others. To overcome this barrier, practice emotional regulation techniques, such as deep breathing or taking a brief pause before responding. Engage in self-care activities that help manage your emotions, allowing you to be more present and receptive to others' communication.

LACK OF EMPATHY: Empathy is a vital component of effective listening and genuine connections. However, our own biases and self-centeredness can hinder our ability to empathize with others. Overcome this barrier by actively practicing empathy. Put yourself in the speaker's shoes, seek to understand their feelings and experiences, and show genuine care and compassion. Cultivate an empathetic mindset by regularly practicing acts of kindness and actively listening to others without judgment.

POOR NON-VERBAL COMMUNICATION: Non-verbal cues, such as body language and facial expressions, play a significant role in effective listening. However, when our non-verbal communication is lacking or contradictory, it can impede genuine connections. Overcome this barrier by improving your non-verbal communication skills. Maintain eye contact, nod and smile to show engagement, and adopt an open and welcoming posture. Pay attention to the speaker's non-verbal cues as well, as they can provide valuable insights into their emotions and intentions.

LACK OF ACTIVE ENGAGEMENT: Passive listening, where we passively absorb information without actively engaging with the speaker, inhibits genuine connections. To overcome this barrier, practice active listening techniques. Ask questions, seek clarification, and provide verbal and non-verbal cues that demonstrate your attentiveness and interest. Engage in reflective listening by paraphrasing and summarizing the speaker's words, which not only deepens understanding but also shows that you value their perspective.

CULTURAL AND LANGUAGE BARRIERS: Cultural and language differences can pose challenges to effective listening and understanding. Overcome these barriers by embracing cultural diversity and seeking to learn about different cultural norms and communication styles. Be patient and respectful when interacting with individuals who speak a different language or have an accent. Ask for clarification when needed and foster an inclusive environment where everyone feels valued and understood.

LACK OF TIME AND PATIENCE: In our fast-paced lives, we often rush conversations and fail to allocate sufficient time for active listening. Overcome this barrier by prioritizing quality over quantity. Dedicate uninterrupted time for meaningful conversations, ensuring that you have enough time to listen attentively and engage fully. Cultivate patience and avoid interrupting or rushing the speaker. Show genuine interest by allowing the conversation to unfold naturally, even if it takes more time than anticipated.

TECHNOLOGY-MEDIATED COMMUNICATION: In an increasingly digital world, technology-mediated communication, such as video calls or messaging platforms, can present barriers to effective listening. Overcome these barriers by adapting your communication style to the medium used. Practice active listening techniques even in virtual settings, such as maintaining eye contact through the camera, using appropriate verbal cues, and being mindful of potential audio delays. Strive to create a technology-enabled environment that promotes genuine connections and effective listening.

By actively identifying and overcoming these barriers, we can enhance our listening skills and foster genuine connections with others. Effective listening enables us to truly understand and connect with people on a deeper level, building relationships based on trust, empathy, and mutual respect. Through continuous practice and self-reflection, we can develop the ability to overcome these barriers and become skilled listeners who forge meaningful connections in all aspects of life.

PRACTICING REFLECTIVE LISTENING TECHNIQUES FOR ENHANCED UNDERSTANDING AND RAPPORT

Reflective listening is a powerful technique that fosters enhanced understanding, empathy, and rapport in communication. By employing this approach, you can actively engage with others, demonstrate genuine interest, and create a supportive environment for open dialogue.

Reflective listening involves paraphrasing or summarizing the speaker's words and emotions to show that you comprehend their message.

Here are some effective techniques to practice reflective listening for enhanced understanding and rapport:

PARAPHRASING: Paraphrasing involves restating the speaker's words in your own words. It demonstrates that you are actively processing the information and seeking clarification. Start by saying, "If I understand correctly..." or "So, what you're saying is..." and then restate the main points or key ideas of what the speaker has expressed. Paraphrasing allows the speaker to confirm your understanding and provides an opportunity for them to clarify or expand on their thoughts.

Example: "If I am comprehending your situation accurately, it seems that you are experiencing a sense of being overwhelmed by your workload and encountering challenges in effectively managing your time. Is that right?"

SUMMARIZING: Summarizing involves briefly recapping the speaker's main points or ideas. It helps consolidate information and provides a clear overview of the conversation. Use phrases like "In summary..." or "So, what I've gathered so far is..." followed by a concise summary of the speaker's key points. Summarizing not only shows that you are actively listening but also helps the speaker feel heard and understood.

Example: "In summary, it seems like you're facing challenges in balancing your personal and professional commitments, and you're looking for strategies to prioritize and create a better work-life balance. Did I capture that correctly?"

REFLECTING EMOTIONS: Reflecting emotions involves acknowledging and validating the speaker's feelings. By identifying and reflecting their emotions back to them, you demonstrate empathy and create a safe space for them to express themselves. Use phrases like "It sounds like you're feeling..." or "I can sense that you're..." followed by the emotion you perceive from their words or tone. Reflecting emotions helps the speaker feel understood and builds rapport.

Example: "It sounds like you're feeling frustrated and disappointed with the lack of progress in the project. Is that accurate?"

CLARIFYING: Clarifying is essential for accurate understanding. When you encounter ambiguous or unclear information, seek clarification by asking open-ended questions. Use phrases like "Could you elaborate on..." or "I'm curious to know more about..." to encourage the speaker to provide additional details or explain their thoughts further. Clarifying ensures that you grasp the full context and nuances of their message, leading to improved understanding.

Example: "Could you elaborate on the specific challenges you've been facing in collaborating with your team members? I'd like to understand more about the dynamics involved."

REFLECTING NON-VERBAL CUES: Reflecting non-verbal cues involves acknowledging and responding to the speaker's body language, facial expressions, and tone of voice. Pay attention to their non-verbal cues, such as nodding, smiling, or mirroring their posture, to convey that you are attuned to their communication on multiple levels. Reflecting non-verbal cues helps establish rapport and creates a sense of connection and understanding.

Example: If the speaker appears excited and passionate while discussing a project, you can respond by saying, "I can see how enthusiastic you are about this initiative. Your excitement is contagious!"

Remember, practicing reflective listening techniques requires genuine attentiveness, patience, and a willingness to understand others. By actively engaging with the speaker, paraphrasing their words, summarizing their ideas, reflecting emotions, clarifying information, and acknowledging non-verbal cues, you can foster enhanced understanding and rapport. These skills contribute to effective communication, stronger relationships, and a supportive environment that encourages open dialogue and mutual respect.

CHAPTER 4

THE POWER OF CURIOSITY AND INQUIRY

Curiosity and inquiry are potent forces that drive human learning, discovery, and growth. They are at the core of our innate desire to understand the world around us and to seek answers to our questions.

Embracing and harnessing the power of curiosity and inquiry can lead to profound personal and professional development. Here are some key aspects that highlight the significance of curiosity and inquiry:

FUELING LEARNING AND KNOWLEDGE: Curiosity is the spark that ignites the thirst for knowledge. It propels us to explore, ask questions, and seek answers. By embracing curiosity, we become active learners, constantly seeking new information and insights. This mindset opens doors to deeper understanding, expands our perspectives, and enriches our knowledge base. Inquiry, on the other hand, is the deliberate process of questioning, investigating, and seeking answers. It encourages critical thinking and active engagement, fostering a deeper level of learning and comprehension.

ENCOURAGING INNOVATION AND PROBLEM-SOLVING: Curiosity and inquiry are essential drivers of innovation and problem-solving. When we approach challenges or gaps in knowledge with a curious mindset, we are more likely to explore alternative solutions and think creatively. By asking thoughtful questions and pursuing answers, we can uncover innovative ideas and develop unique approaches to problem-solving. Curiosity and inquiry challenge the status quo, inspire new perspectives, and lead to breakthroughs in various fields.

FOSTERING PERSONAL GROWTH: Embracing curiosity and inquiry can have a transformative impact on personal growth. By continuously seeking knowledge, exploring new ideas, and questioning assumptions, we expand our understanding of ourselves and the world.

Curiosity helps us remain open-minded, adaptable, and receptive to change. It encourages us to step outside our comfort zones, embrace new experiences, and challenge our own beliefs and biases. Through inquiry, we gain self-awareness, clarify our values, and develop a deeper sense of purpose.

STRENGTHENING RELATIONSHIPS AND COMMUNICATION: Curiosity and inquiry are integral to building strong relationships and fostering effective communication. When we approach others with genuine curiosity, we demonstrate interest, respect, and a willingness to understand their perspectives.

Asking open-ended questions and actively listening to the responses deepens our connections and creates a sense of trust and mutual respect. Curiosity and inquiry help bridge cultural differences, promote empathy, and foster meaningful dialogue, enhancing collaboration and cooperation.

CULTIVATING RESILIENCE AND ADAPTABILITY: Curiosity and inquiry cultivate resilience and adaptability in the face of challenges and change. When we approach setbacks or unfamiliar situations with curiosity, we view them as opportunities for growth and learning.

By asking questions and seeking solutions, we adapt and adjust our strategies, turning obstacles into stepping stones. Curiosity and inquiry empower us to embrace uncertainty, explore different possibilities, and navigate complex situations with a growth-oriented mindset.

ENCOURAGING LIFELONG LEARNING: Curiosity and inquiry are lifelong companions on the journey of continuous learning. They fuel a hunger for knowledge and personal development that transcends formal education.

By embracing curiosity and inquiry, we become lifelong learners, continuously seeking new insights and expanding our understanding. This mindset keeps us intellectually stimulated, adaptable to change, and open to new experiences throughout our lives.

To harness the power of curiosity and inquiry, cultivate an inquisitive mindset. Embrace the unknown, ask questions, and actively seek answers. Be open-minded, challenge assumptions, and explore diverse perspectives. Nurture a love for learning, both inside and outside formal educational settings. Emphasize the importance of curiosity and inquiry in your personal and professional endeavors, and encourage others to do the same. By harnessing these powerful forces, we unlock limitless possibilities for personal growth, innovation, and a deeper understanding of the world around us.

EMBRACING CURIOSITY AS A CATALYST FOR LEARNING AND UNDERSTANDING

Curiosity is a natural human instinct that drives our desire to explore, discover, and learn. It is a powerful catalyst that fuels intellectual growth, enhances understanding, and promotes a lifelong love for learning. By embracing curiosity, we unlock new possibilities, expand our horizons, and deepen our understanding of the world. Here are some key reasons why embracing curiosity is essential for learning and understanding:

IGNITING THE DESIRE TO LEARN: Curiosity is the fuel that ignites the desire to learn. When we are genuinely curious about a subject, we become intrinsically motivated to seek knowledge and understanding. It sparks our interest, encourages active engagement, and propels us to ask questions and seek answers.

Embracing curiosity as a catalyst for learning creates a positive feedback loop, where the more we learn, the more curious we become, and the more we want to learn.

ENCOURAGING EXPLORATION AND DISCOVERY: Curiosity pushes us to explore new ideas, perspectives, and experiences. It drives us to venture into unfamiliar territories and break free from our comfort zones. By embracing curiosity, we become open-minded and willing to challenge our preconceived notions. This mindset of exploration and discovery leads to profound insights, connections between seemingly unrelated concepts, and the discovery of new knowledge.

FOSTERING CRITICAL THINKING: Curiosity encourages critical thinking by challenging assumptions, questioning information, and seeking evidence-based answers. It prompts us to analyze and evaluate information critically, separating fact from fiction. Embracing curiosity as a catalyst for learning strengthens our ability to think critically, make informed judgments, and develop a deeper understanding of complex issues.

CULTIVATING A GROWTH MINDSET: Curiosity is closely linked to a growth mindset—the belief that intelligence and abilities can be developed through effort and learning. When we embrace curiosity, we embrace the belief that there is always more to learn and understand.

We view challenges as opportunities for growth, setbacks as stepping stones, and failures as learning experiences. Curiosity cultivates resilience, perseverance, and a willingness to embrace continuous improvement.

PROMOTING INTERDISCIPLINARY CONNECTIONS: Curiosity knows no boundaries. It transcends disciplinary silos and encourages us to connect ideas and concepts across different fields of knowledge.

By embracing curiosity, we develop a multidisciplinary perspective that allows us to see the interconnectedness of various subjects. This cross-pollination of ideas fosters creativity, innovation, and a more comprehensive understanding of complex phenomena.

ENHANCING EMPATHY AND UNDERSTANDING OF OTHERS: Curiosity extends beyond self-directed learning. It also encompasses a genuine interest in understanding others and their perspectives.

By embracing curiosity about different cultures, backgrounds, and beliefs, we cultivate empathy and deepen our understanding of the human experience. Curiosity opens the door to meaningful connections, respectful dialogue, and a more inclusive and compassionate society.

NURTURING A LIFELONG LOVE FOR LEARNING: Embracing curiosity nurtures a lifelong love for learning. When curiosity becomes an integral part of our mindset, we approach every experience as an opportunity to learn and grow. We seek out new challenges, seek diverse perspectives, and remain intellectually stimulated throughout our lives. Embracing curiosity as a catalyst for learning ensures that our thirst for knowledge and understanding continues to evolve and flourish.

To embrace curiosity as a catalyst for learning and understanding, foster an environment that values questioning, encourages exploration, and supports intellectual curiosity.

Cultivate a sense of wonder and awe, maintain an open mind, and never stop asking "why" or "how." Embrace uncertainty, view challenges as learning opportunities, and seek out diverse sources of information. Embracing curiosity as a lifelong companion will enhance your learning journey, deepen your understanding, and unlock a world of intellectual and personal growth.

CULTIVATING A GROWTH MINDSET TO SEEK NEW KNOWLEDGE AND CHALLENGE ASSUMPTIONS

A growth mindset is a belief system that emphasizes the potential for growth, development, and the power of effort and learning. By cultivating a growth mindset, we can unleash our full potential, embrace challenges, seek new knowledge, and challenge assumptions.

It is a mindset that fuels curiosity, fosters resilience, and promotes a lifelong love for learning.

Here are some key strategies for cultivating a growth mindset to seek new knowledge and challenge assumptions:

EMBRACE CHALLENGES: Shift your perspective to see challenges as valuable opportunities for self-improvement rather than as hindrances. Embrace the mindset that challenges are a chance to learn, develop new skills, and expand your knowledge. Instead of shying away from difficult tasks, approach them with enthusiasm and a willingness to learn from the process.

VALUE EFFORT AND PERSISTENCE: Recognize that effort and persistence are key ingredients for success. Understand that setbacks and failures are part of the learning process. Embrace the idea that through perseverance and continuous effort, you can overcome obstacles, improve your skills, and achieve your goals.

VIEW MISTAKES AS LEARNING OPPORTUNITIES: Adopt a mindset that mistakes are valuable learning opportunities. Rather than being discouraged by failure, see it as a chance to gain insights, refine your approach, and grow. Embrace a non-judgmental attitude towards mistakes and use them as stepping stones on your learning journey.

CULTIVATE CURIOSITY: Nurture your innate sense of curiosity and wonder. Maintain a genuine interest in exploring new ideas, concepts, and perspectives. Curiosity stimulates a thirst for knowledge and encourages you to challenge assumptions, seek answers to questions, and explore new realms of understanding.

SEEK CONTINUOUS LEARNING: Cultivate a love for lifelong learning. Understand that learning is not confined to formal education but is a lifelong journey. Seek out new knowledge, whether through books, courses, podcasts, or interactions with others. Actively pursue opportunities to expand your horizons and deepen your understanding of various subjects.

CHALLENGE ASSUMPTIONS: Challenge the assumptions and beliefs that may be limiting your growth. Be open to questioning long-held beliefs and consider alternative perspectives. Embrace the idea that your current knowledge and understanding are not fixed but can evolve and expand with new insights and experiences.

SURROUND YOURSELF WITH GROWTH-MINDED INDIVIDUALS: Surround yourself with individuals who share a growth mindset and inspire you to seek new knowledge and challenge assumptions. Engage in meaningful discussions and collaborative endeavors with people who encourage your intellectual growth and provide different perspectives.

EMPHASIZE PROCESS OVER OUTCOME: Focus on the process rather than being solely outcome-oriented. Value the learning journey, the effort invested, and the lessons gained along the way. Recognize that growth and understanding are not solely measured by achievements but by the progress made and the knowledge acquired.

CELEBRATE GROWTH AND PROGRESS: Acknowledge and celebrate your growth and progress along your learning journey. Recognize and appreciate the steps you have taken, the skills you have developed, and the knowledge you have gained. Embrace a mindset that values the continuous pursuit of growth rather than solely focusing on the end result.

PRACTICE SELF-REFLECTION: Engage in regular self-reflection to assess your mindset and progress. Reflect on your assumptions, biases, and areas for growth. Use self-reflection as a tool for personal and intellectual development, challenging yourself to seek new knowledge, expand your understanding, and challenge assumptions.

By cultivating a growth mindset, you unlock your potential for continuous learning, personal growth, and the ability to challenge assumptions. Embrace challenges, value effort and persistence, view mistakes as learning opportunities, and nurture your curiosity.

Seek new knowledge, surround yourself with growth-minded individuals, and celebrate your growth and progress. With a growth mindset, you can embark on a lifelong journey of seeking new knowledge, challenging assumptions, and expanding your understanding of the world around you.

UTILIZING EFFECTIVE QUESTIONING TECHNIQUES TO UNCOVER DEEPER INSIGHTS AND PERSPECTIVES

Asking effective questions is a powerful tool for uncovering deeper insights, gaining diverse perspectives, and fostering meaningful conversations. By utilizing appropriate questioning techniques, we can delve beyond surface-level information and discover the underlying motivations, beliefs, and emotions that shape people's thoughts and experiences.

Here are some key strategies for utilizing effective questioning techniques to uncover deeper insights and perspectives:

ASK OPEN-ENDED QUESTIONS: Open-ended questions encourage the speaker to provide detailed, thoughtful responses. These questions cannot be answered with a simple "yes" or "no" and invite the speaker to share more information. Begin questions with words like "what," "how," "why," or "tell me about," allowing the speaker to elaborate and provide deeper insights into their experiences and perspectives.

Example: "What are your thoughts on...?", "How did you come to that conclusion?", or "Tell me about your experience with..."

USE PROBING QUESTIONS: Probing questions encourage the speaker to delve deeper into their thoughts and feelings. They prompt reflection and invite the exploration of underlying motivations, beliefs, or concerns. Probing questions challenge assumptions, encourage critical thinking, and foster a richer understanding of the topic at hand.

Example: "Could you explain your reasoning behind that?", "What factors influenced your decision?", or "Can you provide an example that illustrates your point?"

SEEK CLARIFICATION: When something is unclear or ambiguous, seek clarification through targeted questions. This ensures that you have a complete understanding of the speaker's message and avoids misinterpretation. Ask specific questions to pinpoint the aspects that need further clarification or elaboration.

Example: "Could you clarify what you meant by...?", "I'm not sure I fully understand. Can you explain that in more detail?", or "Could you provide an example to illustrate your point?"

ENCOURAGE REFLECTIVE THINKING: Encourage the speaker to reflect on their thoughts and experiences by asking reflective questions. These questions prompt introspection, self-evaluation, and a deeper exploration of their beliefs and values. Reflective questions can lead to profound insights and a greater understanding of the speaker's motivations and perspectives.

Example: "how does that fit with your personal values? "What did you learn from that experience?", or "What factors contribute to your decision-making process?"

CONSIDER MULTIPLE PERSPECTIVES: Encourage the speaker to consider alternative perspectives by asking questions that challenge their assumptions or biases. These questions broaden the conversation, stimulate critical thinking, and foster a more inclusive and well-rounded discussion.

Example: "have you explored different perspectives on this issue", "How might someone with a different background perceive this situation?", or "What might be some counterarguments to your position?"

PRACTICE ACTIVE LISTENING: Active listening is crucial when utilizing effective questioning techniques. Pay close attention to the speaker's responses, non-verbal cues, and emotions. This allows you to ask follow-up questions that demonstrate your attentiveness, validate their experiences, and encourage them to share more deeply.

Example: "I noticed you mentioned feeling frustrated. Can you elaborate on what specifically led to that frustration?", or "You mentioned a personal experience. How did that shape your perspective?"

CREATE A SAFE AND SUPPORTIVE ENVIRONMENT: Foster an environment where individuals feel comfortable sharing their thoughts and experiences. Establish trust, respect, and non-judgmental communication. Encourage open dialogue and assure individuals that their perspectives are valued. This creates a safe space for them to open up and share deeper insights.

By utilizing effective questioning techniques, we can uncover deeper insights and perspectives. Asking open-ended and probing questions, seeking clarification, encouraging reflective thinking, considering multiple perspectives, practicing active listening, and creating a supportive environment all contribute to fostering meaningful conversations and gaining a more comprehensive understanding of others. Effective questioning not only enhances our own knowledge but also promotes empathy, builds stronger relationships, and fosters a more inclusive and respectful society.

CHAPTER 5

BREAKING DOWN COMMUNICATION BARRIERS

Effective communication is vital for building relationships, fostering understanding, and achieving common goals. However, various barriers can hinder communication and impede the exchange of information. By identifying and addressing these barriers, we can break down obstacles to effective communication and create a more inclusive and collaborative environment.

Here are some key strategies for breaking down communication barriers:

ACTIVE LISTENING: Active listening is the foundation of effective communication. Practice attentive listening, giving your full presence to the speaker. Avoid interrupting, genuinely focus on understanding their message, and provide feedback to show that you are engaged and attentive. Active listening fosters mutual understanding, encourages open dialogue, and creates a space for meaningful exchange.

CLEAR AND CONCISE COMMUNICATION: Use clear and concise language to convey your thoughts and ideas. Avoid jargon, acronyms, or complex terminology that may confuse or alienate others. Be mindful of your tone and body language, ensuring they align with your intended message. Clarity in communication minimizes misunderstandings and enhances overall comprehension.

EMPATHY AND UNDERSTANDING: Foster empathy and understanding by considering the perspectives, emotions, and experiences of others. Put yourself in their shoes, seeking to understand their point of view without judgment. Cultivate a safe and inclusive environment where individuals feel comfortable expressing themselves and are encouraged to share their thoughts openly.

NON-VERBAL COMMUNICATION: Communication extends beyond words and encompasses non-verbal cues, including facial expressions, body language, and gestures, which hold great significance.. Be aware of your non-verbal signals and ensure they are aligned with your intended message. Similarly, pay attention to the non-verbal cues of others, as they can provide additional context and insights into their thoughts and feelings.

ADAPTABILITY AND FLEXIBILITY: Communication styles and preferences can vary across individuals and situations. Be adaptable and flexible in your communication approach. Adjust your tone, style, and method of communication to accommodate the needs and preferences of others. Flexibility promotes effective communication and reduces barriers that may arise from differences in communication styles.

ACTIVE FEEDBACK AND CLARIFICATION: Provide active feedback to ensure clarity and understanding. Summarize and paraphrase the speaker's message to confirm your understanding. Ask clarifying questions to address any uncertainties or ambiguities. Active feedback and clarification demonstrate your commitment to effective communication and enable the speaker to provide additional context or information if needed.

CULTURAL SENSITIVITY: Cultural differences can significantly impact communication. Be mindful of cultural norms, customs, and communication styles when engaging with individuals from diverse backgrounds. Educate yourself about different cultural perspectives and adapt your communication approach to foster inclusivity and respect.

CLEAR COMMUNICATION CHANNELS: Utilize clear communication channels that are accessible and appropriate for the context. Consider the use of written communication, face-to-face conversations, virtual platforms, or other means based on the situation and the needs of the individuals involved. Clear communication channels ensure that information is conveyed effectively and reaches the intended audience.

CONFLICT RESOLUTION SKILLS: Communication barriers can often lead to conflicts or misunderstandings. Develop conflict resolution skills to address conflicts constructively. Practice active listening, empathy, and open-mindedness when resolving conflicts. Seek common ground and find mutually beneficial solutions that promote effective communication and preserve relationships.

CONTINUOUS IMPROVEMENT: Effective communication is an ongoing process of improvement. Reflect on your own communication skills and seek feedback from others. Identify areas for growth and actively work towards enhancing your communication abilities.

Embrace a mindset of continuous learning and improvement to break down communication barriers effectively.

By implementing these strategies, you can break down communication barriers and foster a more inclusive, collaborative, and effective communication environment. Building strong communication skills promotes understanding, strengthens relationships, and creates a foundation for successful collaboration in personal, professional, and societal contexts.

UNDERSTANDING THE NUANCES OF EFFECTIVE COMMUNICATION

Effective communication is a multifaceted process that goes beyond conveying information. It involves understanding the nuances of how messages are sent, received, and interpreted. By recognizing and mastering these nuances, we can enhance our ability to connect with others, convey our thoughts clearly, and foster meaningful interactions.

Here are key aspects to consider when aiming for effective communication:

VERBAL AND NON-VERBAL COMMUNICATION: Communication encompasses both verbal and non-verbal cues. Verbal communication involves the words we choose, tone of voice, and clarity of speech. Non-verbal communication includes body language, facial expressions, gestures, and eye contact. Understanding how these elements work together is crucial for effective communication. Aligning verbal and non-verbal cues ensures that the intended message is conveyed accurately and helps build rapport.

ACTIVE LISTENING: Effective communication involves active listening, which requires focused attention and engagement. Active listening means being fully present, avoiding distractions, and genuinely seeking to understand the speaker's message. It involves observing non-verbal cues, paraphrasing to confirm understanding, and asking relevant questions. By actively listening, we create an environment that encourages open dialogue and deepens mutual understanding.

CONTEXT AND ADAPTABILITY: Effective communication takes into account the context in which it occurs. Consider the cultural, social, and environmental factors that influence communication. Adapt your communication style to suit the situation and the individuals involved. Being adaptable and sensitive to context helps ensure that your message is appropriate and well-received.

CLARITY AND SIMPLICITY: Clear and concise communication is key to effective communication. Avoid using jargon, technical terms, or excessive complexity that may confuse the listener. Use simple language, structure your thoughts logically, and be mindful of the pace at which you speak. Clarity eliminates ambiguity and enhances comprehension.

EMPATHY AND PERSPECTIVE-TAKING: Effective communication requires empathy and the ability to consider other perspectives. Put yourself in the shoes of the listener, seek to understand their feelings and experiences, and respond with empathy. By acknowledging and validating their perspective, you create a safe and respectful space for open dialogue and meaningful connection.

FEEDBACK AND REFLECTION: Effective communication involves providing and receiving feedback. Actively seek feedback to understand how your communication is perceived and make necessary adjustments. Engage in self-examination and analyze your communication style, identifying your strengths and pinpointing areas that could benefit from refinement. Continuous self-reflection and feedback foster growth and refine your communication skills over time.

EMOTIONAL INTELLIGENCE: Emotional intelligence plays a significant role in effective communication. It involves understanding and managing your own emotions and recognizing the emotions of others. Emotional intelligence helps navigate difficult conversations, respond empathetically, and build trust. Developing emotional intelligence enhances your ability to communicate effectively in various situations.

TIMING AND PACING: Effective communication considers timing and pacing. Be mindful of the appropriate time and place for discussions, as well as the pace at which information is conveyed. Adapt your communication style to match the urgency or importance of the topic. Proper timing and pacing contribute to successful communication outcomes.

FEEDBACK AND VALIDATION: Provide feedback and validation to ensure that the intended message is understood. Summarize and paraphrase the speaker's points to demonstrate active listening and confirm understanding. Offer validation by acknowledging the speaker's feelings and perspectives. Effective communication involves building trust and fostering a sense of validation and mutual respect.

CONTINUOUS LEARNING AND IMPROVEMENT: Effective communication is a lifelong learning process. Seek opportunities to develop and refine your communication skills. Stay open to feedback, engage in active self-reflection, and embrace growth. Continuous learning and improvement enable you to adapt to evolving communication needs and enhance your effectiveness in various contexts.

By understanding and considering these nuances, we can communicate more effectively, foster meaningful connections, and bridge gaps in understanding. Effective communication is a skill that can be cultivated through practice, self-awareness, and a commitment to continuous improvement.

OVERCOMING CULTURAL, GENERATIONAL, AND LANGUAGE BARRIERS FOR MEANINGFUL EXCHANGES

Meaningful exchanges require navigating and overcoming barriers that can arise from cultural differences, generational gaps, and language barriers. By recognizing and addressing these challenges, we can foster effective communication, build stronger relationships, and promote mutual understanding.

Here are key strategies for overcoming cultural, generational, and language barriers for meaningful exchanges:

CULTURAL BARRIERS:

- FOSTER CULTURAL AWARENESS: Educate yourself about different cultures, customs, and communication norms. Develop an understanding of cultural sensitivities and adapt your communication style accordingly.

- EMBRACE CULTURAL DIVERSITY: Value and respect diverse perspectives. Seek to learn from others' cultural backgrounds and be open to different ways of thinking and communicating.

- PRACTICE ACTIVE LISTENING: Actively listen and be attentive to non-verbal cues, as they often carry cultural significance. Avoid making assumptions and seek clarification when needed.

GENERATIONAL BARRIERS:

- BRIDGE THE GENERATION GAP: Recognize that different generations may have distinct communication styles and preferences. Be adaptable and flexible in your approach to bridge the generational divide.

- FOSTER INTERGENERATIONAL COLLABORATION: Encourage collaboration and knowledge sharing across generations. Create opportunities for different age groups to work together, fostering mutual learning and understanding.

- EMPHASIZE COMMON GOALS AND VALUES: Focus on shared goals and values to find common ground and build meaningful connections. Highlight areas of alignment rather than differences to foster a sense of unity.

LANGUAGE BARRIERS:

- SIMPLIFY AND CLARIFY: Use simple language and avoid complex terminology or jargon. Speak clearly and at a moderate pace to facilitate understanding. If necessary, provide definitions or explanations to ensure clarity.

- ENCOURAGE TWO-WAY COMMUNICATION: Encourage active participation from all parties involved. Create a supportive environment where individuals feel comfortable asking for clarification or expressing themselves in their non-native language.

Utilize Translation and Interpretation Resources: Use professional translation or interpretation services when necessary to bridge language gaps. Ensure that all parties have equal access to information and can fully participate in the exchange.

SEEK COMMON GROUND:

- FIND SHARED INTERESTS: Discover common interests, goals, or experiences to establish a basis for meaningful exchanges. Look for topics or activities that can bring people together and create a sense of connection.

- FOSTER EMPATHY AND UNDERSTANDING: Practice empathy by putting yourself in the other person's shoes. Seek to understand their perspective and the context that shapes their communication style. This helps build rapport and trust.

PRACTICE PATIENCE AND RESPECT:

- BE PATIENT: Recognize that overcoming barriers takes time and effort. Patience is crucial when working through cultural, generational, or language differences. Allow space for individuals to express themselves and process information at their own pace.

- SHOW RESPECT: Treat others with respect, regardless of their cultural, generational, or language background. Be mindful of cultural norms, generational expectations, and language sensitivities. Avoid making assumptions or judgments based on these differences.

CONTINUOUS LEARNING:

- COMMIT TO LIFELONG LEARNING: Embrace a mindset of continuous learning and improvement. Seek opportunities to develop your intercultural and intergenerational communication skills. Stay open to feedback, engage in self-reflection, and actively seek to expand your knowledge and understanding.

By implementing these strategies, we can overcome cultural, generational, and language barriers and create meaningful exchanges. Effective communication across these differences requires empathy, respect, patience, and a willingness to learn and adapt. By fostering understanding and promoting inclusive communication practices, we build stronger connections, bridge divides, and promote a more harmonious and collaborative society.

DEVELOPING NON-VERBAL COMMUNICATION SKILLS TO ENHANCE UNDERSTANDING AND CONNECTION

Non-verbal communication plays a significant role in our interactions, often conveying messages and emotions that words alone cannot express. By developing and honing our non-verbal communication skills, we can enhance understanding, build stronger connections, and create a more meaningful and authentic communication experience.

Here are key strategies for developing non-verbal communication skills to enhance understanding and connection:

BODY LANGUAGE AWARENESS:

- OBSERVE YOUR OWN BODY LANGUAGE: Pay attention to your own body language and the signals you may be sending. Be aware of your posture, facial expressions, gestures, and movements. Ensure that your body language aligns with the message you want to convey.

- UNDERSTAND CULTURAL DIFFERENCES: Recognize that body language can vary across cultures. Educate yourself about cultural norms and be mindful of how your body language may be perceived in different cultural contexts. Adapt your non-verbal cues to be respectful and considerate of others' cultural backgrounds.

- EMOTE GENUINE EMOTIONS: Practice expressing genuine emotions through your facial expressions. Be mindful of the messages conveyed by your facial cues, such as smiles, frowns, raised eyebrows, or eye contact. Use facial expressions to reflect empathy, understanding, and engagement.

- OBSERVE OTHERS' FACIAL EXPRESSIONS: Pay attention to the facial expressions of others to gauge their emotions and reactions. Notice micro-expressions that may indicate underlying feelings. This helps you respond appropriately and with greater understanding.

EYE CONTACT:

- ESTABLISH EYE CONTACT: Maintain appropriate and comfortable eye contact during conversations. Eye contact conveys interest, attentiveness, and respect. However, be mindful of cultural norms, as eye contact practices can vary across different contexts and individuals.

- ADAPT EYE CONTACT TO THE SITUATION: Adjust your eye contact to the context and individuals involved. In some situations, prolonged eye contact may be appropriate and foster connection. In other scenarios, such as in certain cultural contexts, maintaining more intermittent eye contact may be preferred.

GESTURES AND BODY MOVEMENTS:

- USE PURPOSEFUL GESTURES: Incorporate purposeful and meaningful gestures that complement your verbal communication. Use hand movements, arm gestures, and body language to emphasize key points or convey enthusiasm. However, be aware of excessive or distracting gestures that may detract from your message.

- ADAPT TO DIFFERENT SPACES: Adjust your body movements to suit the space and environment. Be mindful of personal space boundaries and the comfort level of those around you. Adapt your gestures and body movements accordingly to create a sense of connection and respect.

PROXEMICS:

- UNDERSTAND PERSONAL SPACE: Recognize personal space preferences, which can vary among individuals and cultures. Respect others' personal boundaries by maintaining an appropriate distance during conversations. Be attentive to cues of discomfort and adjust your proximity accordingly.

- ADAPT TO CULTURAL NORMS: Be aware of cultural norms regarding personal space. Some cultures may have different expectations for physical proximity during interactions. Adapting to these cultural norms helps create a comfortable and respectful communication environment.

VOICE TONE AND INFLECTION:

- USE VARIED TONE AND INFLECTION: Practice using varied tone and inflection in your speech to convey meaning and emotion. Adjust your voice to match the content and context of your message. Modulate your voice to express enthusiasm, empathy, or authority when appropriate.

- LISTEN TO TONE AND INFLECTION: Pay attention to the tone and inflection of others' voices. Listen for cues of excitement, frustration, or sincerity. Being attuned to vocal nuances enhances your understanding of their emotions and intentions.

ACTIVE LISTENING AND FEEDBACK:

- PRACTICE ACTIVE LISTENING: Actively listen to others by observing their non-verbal cues while they speak. Maintain eye contact, nod to show understanding and engagement, and use appropriate facial expressions to indicate empathy and interest.

- PROVIDE NON-VERBAL FEEDBACK: Use non-verbal cues, such as nods, smiles, or hand gestures, to provide feedback and encourage the speaker. These cues signal that you are actively involved in the conversation and value what is being shared.

REFLECT AND ADAPT:

- REFLECT ON YOUR NON-VERBAL COMMUNICATION: Regularly reflect on your non-verbal communication skills and their impact on your interactions. Identify areas where adjustments can be made and proactively work towards improvement.

- ADAPT TO DIFFERENT INDIVIDUALS: Recognize that individuals may have different non-verbal communication preferences. Adapt your own cues to make others feel comfortable and build stronger connections.

By developing your non-verbal communication skills, you can enhance understanding, foster connection, and create more meaningful interactions. Pay attention to your body language, facial expressions, eye contact, gestures, and voice tone.

Adapt your non-verbal cues to respect cultural differences and individual preferences. Active listening and providing non-verbal feedback further enhance understanding and connection. With practice and awareness, non-verbal communication becomes a powerful tool for building rapport and establishing meaningful connections with others.

CHAPTER 6

THE ROLE OF EMPATHIC LEADERSHIP

Empathic leadership is a style of leadership that emphasizes understanding, connecting with, and considering the perspectives and emotions of others. It is rooted in empathy, the ability to recognize and share in the feelings and experiences of others.

Empathic leaders create a supportive and inclusive environment, foster strong relationships, and inspire their teams to reach their full potential.

Here are key aspects that highlight the role of empathic leadership:

BUILDING TRUST AND CONNECTION: Empathic leaders prioritize building trust and creating a sense of connection with their team members. By demonstrating genuine care and concern, they establish a foundation of trust that allows for open communication and collaboration. Through active listening and understanding, empathic leaders foster a sense of belonging and promote a supportive work culture.

DEVELOPING EMOTIONAL INTELLIGENCE: Emotional intelligence is a core component of empathic leadership. Leaders with high emotional intelligence are able to recognize and manage their own emotions while also understanding and responding to the emotions of others. This skill set allows empathic leaders to navigate complex interpersonal dynamics, diffuse conflicts, and create an emotionally healthy work environment.

PROMOTING COLLABORATION AND TEAMWORK: Empathic leaders recognize the value of collaboration and teamwork. They encourage open dialogue, active participation, and diverse perspectives. By fostering a collaborative atmosphere, empathic leaders harness the collective intelligence of their teams and encourage innovation and creativity.

Supporting Personal and Professional Growth: Empathic leaders prioritize the growth and development of their team members. They take an active interest in understanding individuals' strengths, aspirations, and challenges. Through personalized coaching, mentorship, and support, empathic leaders create opportunities for their team members to thrive, enhancing overall performance and job satisfaction.

ENCOURAGING PSYCHOLOGICAL SAFETY: Empathic leaders cultivate an environment of psychological safety, where individuals feel comfortable taking risks, sharing ideas, and expressing themselves without fear of judgment or negative consequences. By creating a safe space for open communication and vulnerability, empathic leaders foster innovation, collaboration, and continuous learning.

RESOLVING CONFLICTS AND CHALLENGES: Empathic leaders are skilled at conflict resolution and managing challenging situations. They approach conflicts with empathy, seeking to understand the underlying issues and perspectives of all parties involved. Through effective communication, active listening, and problem-solving skills, empathic leaders help resolve conflicts in a constructive manner that preserves relationships and promotes growth.

LEADING WITH PURPOSE AND VALUES: Empathic leaders lead by example, aligning their actions with their values and purpose. They inspire and motivate others by demonstrating authenticity, integrity, and a genuine commitment to the organization's mission. By modeling ethical behavior and fostering a values-driven culture, empathic leaders create a sense of purpose and shared vision among their teams.

ADAPTABILITY AND FLEXIBILITY: Empathic leaders understand the importance of adaptability and flexibility in an ever-changing business landscape. They are open to new ideas, embrace diversity, and are willing to adjust their leadership approach to meet the evolving needs of their team and organization. This adaptability allows empathic leaders to respond effectively to challenges and create a positive and resilient work environment.

ENHANCING EMPLOYEE ENGAGEMENT AND WELL-BEING: Empathic leadership significantly impacts employee engagement and well-being. By demonstrating empathy and understanding, leaders create an environment where individuals feel valued, heard, and supported. This, in turn, leads to higher levels of job satisfaction, increased productivity, and overall well-being among team members.

CREATING A POSITIVE ORGANIZATIONAL CULTURE: Empathic leaders play a crucial role in shaping the organizational culture. By fostering empathy, understanding, and compassion, they contribute to a positive work culture where individuals are encouraged to bring their authentic selves to work. This inclusive culture promotes collaboration, creativity, and a sense of belonging.

Empathic leadership is a powerful approach that prioritizes understanding, connection, and the well-being of team members. By leading with empathy, leaders can create a positive work environment, foster meaningful relationships, and drive organizational success. Ultimately, empathic leadership empowers individuals, promotes growth, and creates a lasting impact on both the individuals and the organization as a whole.

EXPLORING THE IMPACT OF EMPATHIC LEADERSHIP ON TEAMS AND ORGANIZATIONS

Empathic leadership has a profound impact on teams and organizations, creating positive outcomes and fostering a supportive and high-performing work environment. By prioritizing understanding, connection, and the well-being of team members, empathic leaders drive engagement, collaboration, and organizational success.

Here is a comprehensive exploration of the impact of empathic leadership:

ENHANCED EMPLOYEE ENGAGEMENT:

Empathic leadership cultivates higher levels of employee engagement. When leaders demonstrate genuine care, empathy, and understanding, team members feel valued, appreciated, and supported. This emotional connection creates a sense of belonging and loyalty, leading to increased job satisfaction and a deeper commitment to organizational goals.

IMPROVED COLLABORATION AND TEAMWORK:

Empathic leaders promote collaboration and teamwork by fostering open communication and creating a safe environment for sharing ideas. By encouraging active participation and respecting diverse perspectives, they harness the collective intelligence of the team. This collaborative approach leads to increased innovation, better problem-solving, and more effective decision-making.

INCREASED PRODUCTIVITY AND PERFORMANCE:

Empathic leadership positively influences productivity and performance. When employees feel understood and supported, they are more motivated to perform at their best. Empathic leaders provide personalized support, mentorship, and development opportunities, helping team members unlock their full potential. This investment in individual growth and well-being translates into improved overall team performance.

POSITIVE ORGANIZATIONAL CULTURE:

Empathic leadership plays a pivotal role in shaping a positive organizational culture. Leaders who demonstrate empathy create an inclusive and psychologically safe work environment. This culture values open communication, respects diverse perspectives, and encourages collaboration. A positive organizational culture fosters employee satisfaction, reduces turnover, and attracts top talent.

ENHANCED EMPLOYEE WELL-BEING:

Empathic leaders prioritize the well-being of their team members. They demonstrate understanding and provide support during challenging times, acknowledging both personal and professional concerns. By fostering work-life balance, promoting self-care, and creating a positive work environment, empathic leaders contribute to improved employee well-being, reduced stress levels, and increased job satisfaction.

EFFECTIVE CONFLICT RESOLUTION:

Empathic leaders excel in conflict resolution and managing challenging situations. They approach conflicts with empathy and understanding, seeking to find mutually beneficial solutions. By promoting open dialogue, active listening, and respectful communication, empathic leaders resolve conflicts constructively, preserving relationships, and maintaining a harmonious work environment.

HIGHER RETENTION RATES:

Empathic leadership significantly contributes to higher employee retention rates. When leaders show genuine care and understanding, employees are more likely to remain committed to the organization. The positive relationships built through empathic leadership create a sense of loyalty, reducing turnover and the associated costs of recruitment and training.

ENHANCED CUSTOMER SATISFACTION:

Empathic leadership has a ripple effect on customer satisfaction. When employees feel valued and supported, they are more engaged and motivated to provide exceptional customer service. Empathic leaders empower their teams to understand and respond to customer needs with empathy and professionalism, leading to increased customer satisfaction, loyalty, and positive brand perception.

ORGANIZATIONAL ADAPTABILITY:

Empathic leaders foster adaptability and resilience within organizations. By actively listening to employees, staying attuned to their needs, and promoting a culture of open feedback, empathic leaders create an environment where individuals feel comfortable expressing concerns and suggesting improvements. This adaptability allows organizations to respond effectively to changing market conditions and stay ahead of the competition.

SUSTAINABLE PERFORMANCE AND GROWTH:

Empathic leadership lays the foundation for sustainable performance and long-term growth. By nurturing the well-being of team members, promoting collaboration, and creating a positive work culture, empathic leaders foster employee satisfaction and organizational resilience. This, in turn, leads to increased productivity, improved customer relationships, and ultimately, sustained success and growth.

In summary, empathic leadership positively impacts teams and organizations by driving employee engagement, promoting collaboration, enhancing productivity, and shaping a positive work culture. Through effective communication, active listening, and a focus on employee well-being, empathic leaders create a supportive environment that fosters high performance, creativity, and long-term organizational success.

CULTIVATING EMPATHY IN LEADERSHIP TO FOSTER TRUST, COLLABORATION, AND INNOVATION

Empathy is a critical skill for effective leadership, as it fosters trust, collaboration, and innovation within teams and organizations.

Cultivating empathy allows leaders to understand and connect with their team members on a deeper level, creating a supportive environment where individuals feel valued and motivated to contribute their best.

Here is a comprehensive exploration of how cultivating empathy in leadership fosters trust, collaboration, and innovation:

BUILDING TRUST:

Empathy is the foundation of trust. When leaders demonstrate empathy, they show understanding, care, and respect for their team members' experiences and emotions. This creates a safe and supportive environment where individuals feel comfortable expressing themselves, taking risks, and sharing their ideas. Trust is essential for fostering open communication, collaboration, and a sense of psychological safety within the team.

ENHANCING COLLABORATION:

Empathetic leaders foster collaboration by recognizing and valuing the diverse perspectives and strengths of team members. They create an inclusive culture where everyone's input is welcomed and considered. By understanding the needs and motivations of each team member, empathetic leaders can assign tasks, form cross-functional teams, and facilitate effective collaboration that leverages the unique skills and experiences of individuals.

ENCOURAGING INNOVATION:

Empathy in leadership fuels innovation by encouraging individuals to think creatively and take risks. When leaders genuinely understand their team members' challenges and aspirations, they can provide the necessary support and resources to foster innovation. Empathetic leaders create a culture where failures are seen as learning opportunities, and individuals are encouraged to experiment, share ideas, and explore new approaches.

ACTIVE LISTENING:

Cultivating empathy requires active listening. Empathetic leaders practice attentive listening to understand the thoughts, concerns, and perspectives of their team members fully. They give their undivided attention, maintain eye contact, and show genuine interest in what others have to say. Active listening builds trust, enhances communication, and allows leaders to gain valuable insights, leading to better decision-making and problem-solving.

EMOTIONAL INTELLIGENCE:

Developing emotional intelligence is key to cultivating empathy in leadership. Emotionally intelligent leaders can recognize, understand, and manage their own emotions while also empathizing with others.

They are attuned to the emotional needs of their team members and can respond with empathy and sensitivity. Emotional intelligence enables leaders to navigate conflicts, resolve issues, and foster a positive and inclusive work environment.

PERSPECTIVE-TAKING:

Empathetic leaders practice perspective-taking, putting themselves in others' shoes to understand their experiences and viewpoints. By actively considering different perspectives, leaders can make informed decisions, develop comprehensive solutions, and build consensus among team members. Perspective-taking also promotes empathy and understanding, strengthening relationships and collaboration.

AUTHENTICITY AND VULNERABILITY:

Cultivating empathy in leadership involves demonstrating authenticity and vulnerability. Leaders who are open about their own emotions, challenges, and mistakes create a culture where others feel safe to share their own vulnerabilities. This authenticity fosters trust and encourages open communication, allowing for deeper connections and increased collaboration.

EMPLOYEE DEVELOPMENT AND SUPPORT:

Empathetic leaders prioritize the development and well-being of their team members. They take the time to understand each individual's strengths, aspirations, and challenges, providing personalized support and guidance. By showing empathy, leaders can create growth opportunities, offer mentorship, and provide a nurturing environment that fosters individual and team success.

RECOGNITION AND APPRECIATION:

Empathetic leaders acknowledge and appreciate the contributions of their team members. They provide regular feedback and recognition, valuing the efforts and achievements of individuals. This recognition reinforces a sense of value and belonging, motivating team members to continue their innovative and collaborative efforts.

CONTINUOUS LEARNING AND IMPROVEMENT:
Cultivating empathy is an ongoing process. Empathetic leaders continuously seek opportunities to learn, grow, and expand their understanding of different perspectives and experiences. They actively seek feedback from their team members, reflect on their own behaviors and biases, and make adjustments to improve their empathy skills. By modeling a commitment to continuous learning and improvement, leaders inspire their teams to do the same.

In summary, cultivating empathy in leadership fosters trust, collaboration, and innovation. Through active listening, emotional intelligence, perspective-taking, and authenticity, empathetic leaders create a culture where individuals feel valued, motivated, and supported. This culture promotes open communication, creativity, and a sense of psychological safety, leading to increased collaboration, innovation, and ultimately, organizational success.

HARNESSING THE POWER OF UNDERSTANDING TO DRIVE POSITIVE CHANGE IN THE WORKPLACE

Understanding plays a crucial role in driving positive change within the workplace. When leaders and employees prioritize understanding, they create an environment that values empathy, open communication, and collaboration.

By cultivating a deep understanding of diverse perspectives, needs, and challenges, organizations can foster a culture of respect, inclusivity, and continuous improvement.

Here is a comprehensive exploration of how harnessing the power of understanding drives positive change in the workplace:

FOSTERING EMPATHY AND CONNECTION:

Understanding others' experiences and emotions cultivates empathy, fostering a sense of connection among team members. When individuals feel understood and valued, they are more motivated to collaborate, support one another, and work towards common goals. This sense of empathy and connection creates a positive work culture that encourages teamwork and enhances overall job satisfaction.

ENCOURAGING OPEN COMMUNICATION:

Understanding promotes open and honest communication within the workplace. When individuals feel heard and understood, they are more likely to share their thoughts, ideas, and concerns openly. This open communication enables organizations to identify challenges, address issues, and implement necessary changes effectively. It also encourages feedback and fosters a culture of continuous improvement.

VALUING DIVERSITY AND INCLUSION:

Understanding diverse perspectives and experiences allows organizations to value and embrace diversity. When leaders and employees seek to understand different viewpoints, they create an inclusive environment where everyone's voice is respected and heard. Embracing diversity drives innovation, fosters creativity, and leads to more comprehensive decision-making processes.

PROMOTING COLLABORATION AND TEAMWORK:

Understanding fosters collaboration and teamwork. When individuals take the time to understand each other's strengths, challenges, and working styles, they can form effective and cohesive teams. Understanding promotes the sharing of knowledge, the pooling of resources, and the appreciation of different contributions. This collaboration enhances productivity, problem-solving, and overall team performance.

DRIVING CHANGE AND INNOVATION:

Understanding enables organizations to drive change and innovation. By deeply understanding customer needs, market trends, and emerging technologies, organizations can identify opportunities for improvement and develop innovative solutions. Understanding employees' perspectives and aspirations also helps create a supportive environment that encourages creative thinking and risk-taking.

NURTURING EMPLOYEE ENGAGEMENT:

Understanding fosters employee engagement by showing that their contributions and well-being are valued. When leaders and organizations demonstrate an understanding of employees' career goals, work-life balance, and personal development needs, employees are more engaged, motivated, and committed. Engaged employees contribute their best work, leading to improved productivity and organizational success.

RESOLVING CONFLICTS AND BUILDING RESILIENCE:

Understanding plays a vital role in conflict resolution and building resilience. When individuals take the time to understand the underlying causes of conflicts, they can address them effectively and seek mutually beneficial solutions. Understanding also helps build resilience by creating an environment where challenges are viewed as opportunities for growth and learning.

ENHANCING LEADERSHIP EFFECTIVENESS:

Understanding is a critical component of effective leadership. When leaders strive to understand the needs, motivations, and aspirations of their team members, they can provide the necessary support, guidance, and resources. This understanding builds trust, enhances employee development, and enables leaders to adapt their leadership styles to maximize individual and team performance.

SUPPORTING WORK-LIFE BALANCE AND WELL-BEING:

Understanding promotes work-life balance and well-being within the workplace. When organizations and leaders understand the individual needs and responsibilities of their employees, they can provide flexible work arrangements, support resources, and a positive work environment. This understanding contributes to employee well-being, reducing stress, and increasing job satisfaction.

DRIVING CONTINUOUS LEARNING AND IMPROVEMENT: Understanding fosters a culture of continuous learning and improvement. By seeking to understand industry trends, customer feedback, and internal processes, organizations can identify areas for growth and development. Understanding also encourages individuals to embrace a growth mindset, actively seek feedback, and continually enhance their skills and knowledge.

In summary, harnessing the power of understanding drives positive change in the workplace. By fostering empathy, encouraging open communication, valuing diversity, promoting collaboration, and driving change and innovation, organizations create a culture that supports employee engagement, resilience, and continuous learning. Understanding contributes to a positive work environment, improved productivity, and long-term success.

Embracing the power of understanding leads to positive change that benefits individuals, teams, and the organization as a whole.

CHAPTER 7

UNDERSTANDING CONFLICT AND

RESOLVING DIFFERENCES

Conflict is an inevitable part of human interaction, occurring in various settings, including the workplace. However, conflicts, when managed effectively, can lead to growth, innovation, and stronger relationships. Understanding conflict and developing effective strategies to resolve differences is essential for maintaining a harmonious and productive work environment.

Here is a comprehensive exploration of understanding conflict and resolving differences:

UNDERSTANDING CONFLICT:

Conflict arises when there is a perceived or actual disagreement or incompatibility between individuals or groups. It can stem from differences in values, goals, communication styles, or limited resources. Understanding that conflict is a natural and normal part of human interaction helps create a constructive mindset to address and resolve conflicts.

IDENTIFYING CONFLICT STYLES:

Individuals may have different styles of approaching and handling conflicts. Common conflict styles include avoiding, accommodating, competing, compromising, and collaborating. Understanding these styles helps individuals recognize their own tendencies and adapt their approach to fit the situation, fostering effective conflict resolution.

ACTIVE LISTENING AND EFFECTIVE COMMUNICATION:

Active listening plays a vital role in effectively resolving conflicts. It involves fully focusing on and understanding the perspectives, concerns, and emotions expressed by all parties involved. Active listening promotes empathy and helps build rapport, allowing individuals to communicate their needs, interests, and concerns more effectively.

SEEKING COMMON GROUND:

Identifying areas of agreement or shared goals helps create a foundation for resolving differences. By focusing on common ground, individuals can work together to find mutually beneficial solutions and move beyond the areas of disagreement. Seeking common ground fosters collaboration and builds trust among conflicting parties.

MANAGING EMOTIONS:

Emotional intelligence plays an important and crucial role in conflict resolution. Understanding and managing one's own emotions, as well as recognizing and empathizing with the emotions of others, can help de-escalate conflicts. Emotional regulation and creating a safe space for expressing emotions constructively contribute to more productive conversations.

GENERATING CREATIVE SOLUTIONS:

Resolving differences often involves finding creative solutions that meet the underlying needs and interests of all parties. Encouraging brainstorming and generating alternative options promote innovation and allow for win-win outcomes. Creative problem-solving encourages individuals to think outside the box and consider perspectives beyond their own.

BUILDING TRUST AND RAPPORT:

Trust is essential for resolving conflicts effectively. Building trust requires open and honest communication, keeping commitments, and demonstrating integrity. Establishing rapport through empathy, active listening, and respect helps create a safe and collaborative environment where conflicts can be addressed constructively.

MEDIATION AND FACILITATION:

In complex conflicts, involving a neutral third party as a mediator or facilitator can be beneficial. Mediators help facilitate dialogue, manage power imbalances, and guide conflicting parties toward resolution. Their neutral perspective and facilitation skills enable them to help individuals find common ground and develop mutually acceptable solutions.

LEARNING FROM CONFLICTS:

Conflicts provide opportunities for growth and learning. Reflecting on conflicts and the underlying causes can help individuals and organizations identify patterns, underlying issues, and areas for improvement. By learning from conflicts, individuals can develop better conflict management skills and create systems or processes to prevent similar conflicts in the future.

COMMITMENT TO CONTINUOUS IMPROVEMENT:

Resolving differences is an ongoing process that requires a commitment to continuous improvement. Encouraging a culture of open communication, constructive feedback, and conflict resolution skills development allows individuals and teams to learn from conflicts and enhance their conflict resolution abilities over time.

In summary, understanding conflict and resolving differences is essential for maintaining a healthy and productive work environment. By actively listening, seeking common ground, managing emotions, generating creative solutions, building trust, and utilizing mediation when necessary, individuals and organizations can navigate conflicts constructively.

Embracing conflicts as opportunities for growth and learning contributes to stronger relationships, increased innovation, and a more harmonious work environment.

GAINING INSIGHTS INTO THE ROOT CAUSES OF CONFLICT AND MISUNDERSTANDINGS

Conflict and misunderstandings can often be traced back to underlying causes and factors that, when understood, can pave the way for effective resolution. By gaining insights into the root causes of conflict and misunderstandings, individuals and organizations can address the core issues and work towards sustainable solutions.

Here is a comprehensive exploration of gaining insights into the root causes of conflict and misunderstandings:

COMMUNICATION BREAKDOWN:

Poor communication or miscommunication is a common root cause of conflicts and misunderstandings. Issues may arise from differences in communication styles, lack of clarity in expressing ideas, or the use of ambiguous language. Identifying communication breakdowns and seeking to improve communication channels can help prevent or resolve conflicts.

DIFFERENCES IN VALUES AND BELIEFS:

Conflicts often stem from differences in values, beliefs, and principles. Individuals or groups may have contrasting perspectives, priorities, or expectations. Recognizing and respecting these differences is crucial for understanding the root causes of conflict. Open dialogue, active listening, and empathy can help bridge these gaps and foster understanding.

DIFFERING GOALS AND INTERESTS:

Conflicting goals and interests can lead to misunderstandings and conflicts. When individuals or teams have competing objectives or limited resources, tensions may arise. Identifying these conflicting goals and finding common ground or mutually beneficial solutions is essential to resolving the root causes of conflict.

LIMITED RESOURCES:

Scarcity of resources, such as time, budget, or personnel, can contribute to conflicts. When there is a perceived or actual scarcity, individuals or teams may compete or engage in power struggles. Understanding the constraints and finding equitable ways to allocate resources can mitigate conflicts arising from resource limitations.

PERCEIVED OR ACTUAL INEQUITIES:

Conflict can arise when individuals or groups perceive or experience inequities in treatment, rewards, or opportunities. Recognizing and addressing these disparities is vital for resolving conflicts rooted in inequity. Promoting fairness, transparency, and inclusive practices can help mitigate these conflicts.

PERSONALITY CLASHES:

Personality differences can lead to conflicts and misunderstandings. Individuals with different communication styles, problem-solving approaches, or decision-making preferences may clash. Understanding personality differences and leveraging diverse strengths can promote collaboration and reduce conflicts arising from personality clashes.

CULTURAL AND DIVERSITY ISSUES:

Conflicts may emerge due to cultural misunderstandings or insensitivity to diversity. Cultural norms, values, and communication styles can vary widely. Recognizing and appreciating cultural differences and promoting inclusive practices can help minimize misunderstandings and foster a harmonious work environment.

LACK OF TRUST:

Conflict can be rooted in a lack of trust among individuals or teams. Trust is essential for effective collaboration, open communication, and resolving conflicts. Identifying the lack of trust and taking steps to build trust through transparency, consistency, and relationship-building can help address the root causes of conflict.

POWER DYNAMICS:

Conflicts can arise from power imbalances within the organization. When there is an imbalance of power or perceived unfairness in decision-making processes, conflicts may occur. Understanding power dynamics and promoting participatory decision-making and equitable practices can mitigate conflicts rooted in power struggles.

EXTERNAL FACTORS:

External factors, such as changes in the industry, economic pressures, or external competition, can contribute to conflicts within organizations. Recognizing these external influences and their impact on internal dynamics is important in understanding the root causes of conflict. Adapting to external changes and fostering resilience can help mitigate conflicts arising from external factors.

Gaining insights into the root causes of conflict and misunderstandings requires active listening, open-mindedness, and a commitment to understanding multiple perspectives. It involves creating a safe space for open dialogue, promoting inclusivity, and addressing issues proactively. By understanding the underlying causes, individuals and organizations can develop targeted strategies for conflict resolution, foster a positive work culture, and build stronger relationships.

APPLYING CONFLICT RESOLUTION STRATEGIES BASED ON UNDERSTANDING AND EMPATHY

Conflict resolution strategies rooted in understanding and empathy are essential for addressing conflicts effectively and promoting positive outcomes. By approaching conflicts with empathy and seeking to understand the perspectives and emotions of all parties involved, individuals and organizations can work towards mutually beneficial resolutions.

Here is a comprehensive exploration of applying conflict resolution strategies based on understanding and empathy:

FOSTER OPEN COMMUNICATION:

Encourage open and honest communication to create a safe space for all parties to express their concerns, interests, and emotions. Active listening is crucial in this process, allowing individuals to truly understand and empathize with the viewpoints of others. Establishing clear communication channels promotes constructive dialogue and helps uncover underlying issues.

PRACTICE EMPATHY:

Cultivate empathy by putting yourself in the shoes of others involved in the conflict. Seek to understand their emotions, needs, and motivations. Empathy enables individuals to see beyond their own perspectives, leading to more effective problem-solving and collaboration. Show empathy through verbal and non-verbal cues, such as validating emotions and using reflective statements.

IDENTIFY THE UNDERLYING ISSUES:

Look beyond the surface-level disagreements to identify the root causes and underlying issues contributing to the conflict. This requires active listening, asking clarifying questions, and seeking common ground. By understanding the deeper motivations and concerns of all parties, you can address the underlying issues more effectively.

COLLABORATIVE PROBLEM-SOLVING:

Encourage collaborative problem-solving where all parties work together towards a mutually acceptable solution. Create a space for brainstorming ideas and generating multiple options. By involving all stakeholders in the process, you can tap into the collective wisdom and creativity of the group. Focus on win-win solutions that address the needs and interests of all parties involved.

SEEK MEDIATION OR FACILITATION:

In instances of intricate or intensified conflicts, it is advisable to engage an impartial third party as a mediator or facilitator. A mediator can help guide the conversation, ensure fairness, and promote effective communication. They can create an environment conducive to understanding, empathy, and resolution.

Mediators help parties navigate the conflict and work towards finding common ground.

ENCOURAGE COMPROMISE AND FLEXIBILITY:

Recognize that compromise is often necessary for conflict resolution. Encourage individuals to be flexible and open to finding middle ground. Emphasize the importance of prioritizing the collective goals and relationships over personal interests. A willingness to adapt and find mutually beneficial solutions is essential for resolving conflicts based on understanding and empathy.

MANAGE EMOTIONS:

Emotions can escalate conflicts, making it challenging to achieve resolution. Encourage individuals to manage their emotions constructively, taking breaks if needed to regain composure. Provide support and guidance on emotional regulation techniques, such as deep breathing or reframing negative thoughts. By addressing emotions and maintaining a calm and respectful environment, conflicts can be resolved more effectively.

FOCUS ON LONG-TERM RELATIONSHIPS:

Emphasize the importance of maintaining positive relationships beyond the current conflict. Encourage individuals to consider the impact of their actions on future collaborations and the overall work environment. By prioritizing long-term relationships, individuals are motivated to find resolutions that preserve trust and goodwill.

LEARN FROM CONFLICT:

Conflict provides opportunities for growth and learning. Encourage individuals to reflect on the conflict and identify lessons that can be applied to future situations. This reflection helps individuals develop conflict resolution skills and contributes to a culture of continuous improvement.

IMPLEMENT FEEDBACK AND FOLLOW-UP:

After reaching a resolution, implement mechanisms to gather feedback and evaluate the effectiveness of the solution. Monitor the progress and ensure that the resolution is implemented consistently. Regularly revisit the issue to ensure that any lingering concerns or new conflicts are addressed promptly.

Applying conflict resolution strategies based on understanding and empathy is crucial for effective conflict resolution. By fostering open communication, practicing empathy, identifying underlying issues, promoting collaborative problem-solving, and managing emotions, individuals and organizations can work towards resolutions that preserve relationships and drive positive outcomes. Emphasizing compromise, long-term relationships, and continuous learning further supports the application of conflict resolution strategies rooted in understanding and empathy.

NAVIGATING CHALLENGING CONVERSATIONS AND TRANSFORMING CONFLICT INTO GROWTH OPPORTUNITIES

Challenging conversations and conflicts are inevitable in both personal and professional settings. However, by navigating these conversations with skill and intention, individuals and organizations can transform conflicts into valuable growth opportunities.

Here is a comprehensive exploration of navigating challenging conversations and transforming conflict into growth opportunities:

APPROACH WITH OPENNESS AND CURIOSITY:

Enter challenging conversations with an open mindset and a genuine curiosity to understand different perspectives. Let go of preconceived notions or judgments and be receptive to new information. This mindset creates an atmosphere conducive to productive dialogue and paves the way for growth.

ACTIVE LISTENING AND EMPATHY:

Engage in active listening to truly understand the concerns, emotions, and needs of all parties involved. Show empathy by validating their experiences and demonstrating a genuine desire to understand their point of view. Active listening and empathy foster trust and create an environment where individuals feel heard and respected.

MANAGE EMOTIONS:

Emotions can escalate conflicts and hinder effective communication. Practice emotional intelligence by recognizing and managing your own emotions, as well as understanding and empathizing with the emotions of others. Take breaks if needed to regain composure and approach the conversation with a calm and respectful demeanor.

CHOOSE THE RIGHT TIME AND PLACE:

Consider the timing and setting for the conversation. Find a neutral and private space where all parties can feel comfortable and safe to express themselves. Avoid time pressures or distractions that may hinder open and focused communication.

CLARIFY AND SHARE INTENTIONS:

Clarify your intentions and purpose for the conversation to ensure all parties understand the desired outcome. Share your intentions openly and transparently to build trust and create a shared understanding of the conversation's goals.

FOCUS ON INTERESTS, NOT POSITIONS:

Move beyond entrenched positions and delve into the underlying interests and needs of all parties. Encourage open exploration of interests to uncover common ground and shared goals. Shifting the focus from positions to interests promotes collaboration and opens up possibilities for mutually beneficial solutions.

PRACTICE CONSTRUCTIVE FEEDBACK:

Provide constructive feedback by offering specific examples, focusing on behaviors, and expressing your observations and feelings without blame or judgment. Use "I" statements to convey your perspective and create a non-threatening environment for dialogue.

EXPLORE CREATIVE SOLUTIONS:

Encourage brainstorming and the exploration of alternative solutions. Foster a creative and collaborative atmosphere where individuals can freely share their ideas. Engage in joint problem-solving to generate innovative solutions that address the underlying concerns and interests of all parties.

SEEK MEDIATION OR FACILITATION:

In situations where emotions are high or communication breakdowns persist, consider involving a neutral third party as a mediator or facilitator. Mediators help guide the conversation, ensure fair participation, and support constructive communication. Their impartial perspective can help navigate impasses and transform conflicts into growth opportunities.

REFLECT AND LEARN:

After the challenging conversation, take time to reflect on the outcomes and lessons learned. Evaluate what worked well and areas for improvement. Embrace the conflict as a growth opportunity for personal and professional development, and integrate the insights gained into future interactions.

FOSTER A LEARNING CULTURE:

Encourage a learning culture within the organization where individuals view conflicts as opportunities for growth and learning. Emphasize the importance of feedback, continuous improvement, and open dialogue. Recognize and reward individuals who handle challenging conversations effectively and contribute to the growth and development of the organization.

FOLLOW-UP AND IMPLEMENT CHANGES:

Ensure that the resolutions or agreements reached in challenging conversations are implemented effectively. Establish mechanisms for monitoring progress and provide support to ensure sustained changes. Regularly check in on the outcomes of the conversation and address any new concerns that may arise.

Navigating challenging conversations and transforming conflict into growth opportunities requires a thoughtful and intentional approach. By approaching conversations with openness, active listening, empathy, and a focus on interests, individuals can create an environment conducive to constructive dialogue.

Seeking mediation when needed, reflecting on outcomes, and fostering a learning culture further support the transformation of conflicts into valuable growth opportunities.

Embracing these strategies enables individuals and organizations to build stronger relationships, drive innovation, and enhance overall performance.

CHAPTER 8

FOSTERING UNDERSTANDING IN A DIVERSE WORLD

Fostering understanding in a diverse world is an essential and ongoing process that involves promoting empathy, respect, and inclusivity among individuals from different cultural, ethnic, religious, and socioeconomic backgrounds. In a globalized society where interactions between diverse groups are increasingly common, it is crucial to develop strategies and initiatives that encourage mutual understanding and appreciation, while dismantling prejudices and biases.

One of the fundamental pillars of fostering understanding is education. Educational institutions, from schools to universities, play a significant role in shaping individuals' perspectives and attitudes towards diversity. By incorporating diverse perspectives, histories, and contributions into curricula, students can develop a more comprehensive worldview and challenge stereotypes. It is important to teach cultural competence, promote intercultural communication skills, and provide opportunities for students to engage with diverse communities through field trips, cultural exchange programs, and collaborative projects. Such initiatives can help students develop empathy, respect, and an appreciation for the richness that diversity brings to society.

In addition to formal education, creating spaces for meaningful interactions and dialogue among individuals from different backgrounds is crucial for fostering understanding. Social and cultural events, workshops, and community programs serve as platforms where people can come together, share their experiences, and learn from one another. Building bridges of communication and trust through such initiatives is essential in breaking down barriers and nurturing mutual respect.

The media, including traditional outlets and online platforms, also has a significant role to play in fostering understanding in a diverse world. Media plays a powerful role in shaping public perceptions and influencing attitudes towards different cultures and communities. Responsible media practices that prioritize accurate representation, avoid stereotyping, and promote positive narratives can have a profound impact on shaping public opinion. Media outlets should strive to provide diverse voices and perspectives, ensuring that marginalized communities are not further marginalized by biased reporting or underrepresentation.

Government policies and initiatives are critical in creating an environment that fosters understanding and promotes inclusivity. Governments should enact and enforce anti-discrimination laws that protect the rights of all individuals, regardless of their background. They should also support organizations and initiatives that promote diversity and inclusion, providing funding and resources to programs that aim to bridge gaps between communities. Additionally, promoting diversity in leadership positions and decision-making processes within government institutions ensures that different perspectives are considered, leading to more inclusive policies and practices.

At an individual level, fostering understanding requires a commitment to personal growth and actively challenging one's own biases and assumptions. Engaging in open-minded conversations, actively listening to others' experiences, and being willing to learn and unlearn are essential steps towards fostering understanding. Developing empathy and cultural sensitivity can be achieved by seeking out opportunities to engage with diverse communities, attending cultural events, and participating in intercultural dialogue. It is important to respect and value the differences that make each individual unique, while recognizing our shared humanity.

Fostering understanding in a diverse world is a complex and ongoing process that involves multiple stakeholders and requires continuous effort. Education, meaningful interactions, responsible media practices, government policies, and individual actions all play integral roles. By embracing diversity, challenging prejudices, promoting empathy, and actively seeking opportunities to learn from and about different cultures and perspectives, we can contribute to building a more inclusive, equitable, and harmonious world.

EMBRACING DIVERSITY AND INCLUSION AS CATALYSTS FOR UNDERSTANDING

Embracing diversity and inclusion as catalysts for understanding is a powerful approach that promotes empathy, respect, and harmony in a multifaceted world. By recognizing and appreciating the unique qualities and perspectives that individuals from different backgrounds bring, we can foster a deeper understanding of one another and build inclusive societies that thrive on diversity.

Embracing diversity starts with acknowledging the richness that comes from a range of cultural, ethnic, religious, and socioeconomic backgrounds. Each individual brings a unique set of experiences, values, and knowledge shaped by their heritage and upbringing. By recognizing and valuing these differences, we create an environment that celebrates diversity rather than fearing or rejecting it. Embracing diversity also requires challenging and dismantling biases, stereotypes, and prejudices that can hinder understanding and hinder meaningful connections.

Inclusion goes hand in hand with embracing diversity, as it ensures that individuals from all backgrounds are welcomed, respected, and provided equal opportunities to participate and contribute. Inclusive environments recognize the importance of representation and actively work to overcome barriers that may prevent certain groups from fully participating. This includes creating inclusive policies, practices, and spaces that foster a sense of belonging and enable everyone to thrive. When individuals feel valued, heard, and included, they are more likely to engage in open and honest dialogue, leading to a deeper understanding of one another.

By embracing diversity and inclusion, we create a fertile ground for understanding. Here's how diversity and inclusion act as catalysts for understanding:

BROADENING PERSPECTIVES: Interacting with individuals from diverse backgrounds exposes us to a wide range of perspectives, ideas, and ways of life. It challenges our preconceived notions and encourages us to see the world through different lenses. By embracing diversity, we expand our understanding of the complexities and nuances that exist within the human experience.

ENCOURAGING EMPATHY: When we embrace diversity, we develop empathy by actively seeking to understand and relate to the experiences and challenges faced by individuals from different backgrounds. Empathy allows us to connect on a deeper level, fostering a sense of compassion and understanding for the struggles and triumphs of others.

BREAKING DOWN STEREOTYPES AND PREJUDICES: Diversity and inclusion provide opportunities to challenge stereotypes and prejudices that may be ingrained in our society. By engaging with individuals from diverse backgrounds, we realize that no single narrative can capture the full richness and diversity of a group. This helps to dismantle harmful stereotypes and encourages us to view individuals as unique and complex human beings.

BUILDING BRIDGES OF COLLABORATION: Embracing diversity and inclusion creates opportunities for collaboration and cooperation across different backgrounds. When people with diverse perspectives come together to solve problems or work towards common goals, innovative solutions emerge.

Collaboration across diverse groups fosters understanding as individuals learn from one another and recognize the value of different viewpoints.

CULTIVATING CULTURAL INTELLIGENCE: Embracing diversity allows us to develop cultural intelligence, which is the ability to understand, appreciate, and adapt to different cultural norms and practices. Cultural intelligence enables effective cross-cultural communication, reduces misunderstandings, and builds bridges between communities. It promotes respect and understanding by recognizing and valuing the uniqueness of each culture.

Embracing diversity and inclusion serves as a catalyst for understanding by fostering empathy, broadening perspectives, breaking down stereotypes, building collaboration, and cultivating cultural intelligence. When we embrace and celebrate the richness of diverse backgrounds, we create an environment that encourages meaningful connections and paves the way for a more inclusive and understanding world. By recognizing the inherent value of every individual, we can collectively work towards creating a society that thrives on the strength and beauty of diversity.

BUILDING CULTURAL COMPETENCY TO NAVIGATE AND APPRECIATE DIFFERENT PERSPECTIVES

Building cultural competency is a crucial skill set that allows individuals to navigate and appreciate different perspectives in an increasingly diverse world. Cultural competency refers to the ability to understand, respect, and effectively interact with people from diverse cultural backgrounds. It involves developing knowledge, attitudes, and skills that enable individuals to engage with others in a culturally sensitive and inclusive manner. By building cultural competency, we can foster deeper understanding, bridge gaps, and promote harmonious relationships across cultural boundaries.

DEVELOPING KNOWLEDGE: Cultural competency begins with acquiring knowledge about different cultures, traditions, values, and historical contexts. It involves learning about the diversity within and between cultures, including aspects such as language, customs, beliefs, and social norms. By educating ourselves about various cultures, we gain a foundation for understanding and appreciating different perspectives.

CHALLENGING ASSUMPTIONS AND BIASES: Cultural competency requires recognizing and challenging our own assumptions, biases, and stereotypes. We all have implicit biases that influence our perceptions and interactions. It is important to reflect on these biases and consciously work towards overcoming them. By questioning our preconceived notions, we create space for openness and genuine curiosity about others.

PRACTICING ACTIVE LISTENING: Effective communication is a fundamental aspect of cultural competency. Active listening involves paying attention to verbal and non-verbal cues, seeking clarification, and demonstrating empathy. By truly listening to others, we can better understand their perspectives, experiences, and values. Active listening also helps to build trust and establish meaningful connections.

DEVELOPING EMPATHY AND PERSPECTIVE-TAKING: Empathy is a key element of cultural competency. It involves putting ourselves in someone else's shoes and understanding their emotions, experiences, and challenges. By developing empathy, we can foster a deeper appreciation for the diverse perspectives that people from different cultures bring. Perspective-taking allows us to understand the world from multiple viewpoints, leading to a more nuanced understanding of cultural differences.

ADAPTING COMMUNICATION STYLES: Cultural competency entails adapting our communication styles to accommodate cultural differences. Different cultures have varying norms and expectations regarding communication, such as directness, use of gestures, or level of formality. By being flexible and respectful in our communication approach, we can bridge communication gaps and ensure effective and meaningful interactions.

RESPECTING DIVERSITY AND PROMOTING INCLUSION: Cultural competency involves recognizing and respecting the value of diversity. It means embracing differences and creating inclusive environments where all individuals feel welcomed and valued. By promoting inclusivity, we encourage diverse perspectives to be heard, fostering an environment that nurtures understanding and collaboration.

SEEKING CULTURAL IMMERSION AND EXPERIENCES: Immersing one in different cultural experiences can significantly enhance cultural competency. This may involve participating in cultural events, engaging in cross-cultural exchanges, or traveling to different regions of the world. By actively seeking these experiences, we gain firsthand insights into different cultures, challenge our assumptions, and broaden our perspectives.

CONTINUOUS LEARNING AND SELF-REFLECTION: Building cultural competency is an ongoing process that requires a commitment to lifelong learning and self-reflection. Cultures evolve, and new perspectives emerge, so it is crucial to stay informed and open to learning. Regular self-reflection allows us to assess our growth, identify areas for improvement, and continually develop our cultural competency skills.

Building cultural competency is essential for navigating and appreciating different perspectives in a diverse world. By developing knowledge, challenging biases, practicing active listening, empathy, and perspective-taking, adapting communication styles, promoting inclusion, seeking cultural experiences, and engaging in continuous learning, we can enhance our ability to connect with and understand individuals from diverse cultural backgrounds. Cultural competency serves as a bridge that promotes mutual respect, fosters understanding, and paves the way for meaningful cross-cultural interactions.

ADVOCATING FOR SOCIAL JUSTICE AND EQUALITY THROUGH THE LENS OF UNDERSTANDING

Advocating for social justice and equality through the lens of understanding is a powerful approach that fosters empathy, compassion, and inclusivity. Understanding the experiences, struggles, and aspirations of marginalized communities is crucial in addressing systemic injustices and working towards a more equitable society. By advocating for social justice with a foundation of understanding, we can amplify marginalized voices, challenge oppressive systems, and promote lasting change.

EDUCATING ONESELF: Advocating for social justice begins with self-education. It is essential to understand the historical context, systemic inequalities, and intersectional dynamics that contribute to various forms of oppression. By studying and learning about the experiences and perspectives of marginalized communities, we can develop a deeper understanding of the challenges they face and the root causes of social injustice.

LISTENING TO MARGINALIZED VOICES: To advocate effectively, it is important to center the voices and experiences of marginalized communities. Listening to their stories, concerns, and demands provides insight into their realities and enables us to amplify their voices. By giving space for marginalized individuals to share their experiences and actively listening to their perspectives, we can gain a more nuanced understanding of the issues at hand.

EMPATHY AND PERSPECTIVE-TAKING: Empathy is a cornerstone of understanding and social justice advocacy. It involves putting ourselves in the shoes of others, acknowledging their pain, and recognizing the systemic barriers they face. By cultivating empathy and practicing perspective-taking, we can develop a deeper understanding of the impacts of social injustices and the urgent need for change.

CHALLENGING BIASES AND STEREOTYPES: Advocating for social justice requires actively challenging our own biases and stereotypes. Prejudices can cloud our understanding and perpetuate harmful narratives. By critically examining our assumptions, confronting our biases, and working to unlearn harmful beliefs, we create space for a more inclusive and empathetic worldview.

ENGAGING IN DIALOGUE AND FOSTERING UNDERSTANDING: Meaningful dialogue plays a crucial role in advocating for social justice. By engaging in conversations with individuals from diverse backgrounds, we can foster understanding, bridge gaps, and dismantle misconceptions. Constructive dialogue allows for the exchange of ideas, the exploration of different perspectives, and the building of coalitions to address systemic issues collectively.

INTERSECTIONALITY: Understanding and acknowledging intersectionality is vital in advocating for social justice. Recognizing that individuals can experience multiple forms of oppression and discrimination based on their race, gender, sexuality, ability, and other identities helps us understand the interconnected nature of social injustices. By considering the intersecting dimensions of identity and oppression, we can develop more inclusive and comprehensive approaches to advocacy.

COLLABORATIVE EFFORTS AND ALLYSHIP: Advocating for social justice necessitates collaborative efforts and allyship. Understanding that our own privileges can be used to amplify marginalized voices and advocate for change is crucial. By actively supporting and standing in solidarity with marginalized communities, we can work together to challenge oppressive systems, policies, and practices.

PROMOTING SYSTEMIC CHANGE: Advocacy for social justice aims to create systemic change by addressing root causes of inequality. This requires addressing policies, laws, and practices that perpetuate social injustices. By understanding the structural nature of inequality, we can advocate for transformative change, such as advocating for equitable legislation, promoting inclusive policies, and supporting initiatives that challenge systemic biases.

Advocating for social justice and equality through the lens of understanding is an empathetic and inclusive approach that drives positive change. By educating ourselves, listening to marginalized voices, cultivating empathy, challenging biases, engaging in dialogue, embracing intersectionality, practicing allyship, and working towards systemic change, we can advocate effectively for social justice. Through understanding, we can create a more equitable society that upholds the rights and dignity of all individuals, regardless of their backgrounds.

CHAPTER NINE

THE RIPPLE EFFECT: UNDERSTANDING FOR GLOBAL IMPACT

Understanding plays a critical role in creating a ripple effect of positive change on a global scale. When individuals strive to understand and empathize with one another, it fosters a deeper connection and promotes unity amidst diversity. This understanding, in turn, has the potential to create a ripple effect that transcends boundaries, cultures, and nations, leading to meaningful global impact. By cultivating understanding, we can address complex challenges, bridge divides, and work towards a more harmonious and equitable world.

BUILDING BRIDGES ACROSS CULTURES: Understanding is the foundation upon which bridges are built between individuals from different cultures. By seeking to understand and appreciate diverse cultural perspectives, customs, and traditions, we can break down barriers and forge connections. This bridges the gap of misunderstanding, paving the way for collaboration, mutual respect, and shared learning.

NURTURING EMPATHY AND COMPASSION: Understanding fosters empathy and compassion, enabling individuals to connect with the experiences and struggles of others. When we seek to understand the realities faced by people around the world, it deepens our compassion and motivates us to take action. This empathy fuels efforts to address social, economic, and environmental challenges that impact communities globally.

CHALLENGING STEREOTYPES AND BIASES: Understanding empowers us to challenge stereotypes and biases that hinder progress. It prompts us to question assumptions and misconceptions, leading to a more nuanced understanding of diverse individuals and cultures. By dismantling stereotypes, we contribute to creating inclusive spaces where everyone's voice is valued, and prejudices are diminished.

FOSTERING EFFECTIVE COMMUNICATION: Understanding enhances communication by facilitating effective dialogue. When we strive to understand others' perspectives, we are better equipped to communicate respectfully and constructively. This fosters collaboration, enables the exchange of ideas, and cultivates innovative solutions to global problems.

PROMOTING PEACE AND CONFLICT RESOLUTION: Understanding is a fundamental element in promoting peace and resolving conflicts. By seeking to understand the root causes of conflicts, the underlying grievances, and the aspirations of all parties involved, we can facilitate dialogue and negotiations. This leads to sustainable peace-building efforts and reduces the likelihood of future conflicts.

ADVANCING GLOBAL COOPERATION: Understanding is instrumental in fostering global cooperation and partnerships. When individuals and nations seek to understand one another's interests, needs, and values, it paves the way for collaborative efforts to address shared challenges. Global cooperation on issues such as climate change, poverty alleviation, and public health is essential for creating impactful change on a global scale.

INSPIRING INDIVIDUAL ACTIONS: Understanding inspires individuals to take action in their own spheres of influence. When we understand the interconnectedness of our actions and their impact on others, we become more conscious of the choices we make. This leads to individual actions that promote sustainability, social justice, and equality, creating a cumulative effect of positive change.

ENCOURAGING RESPONSIBLE GLOBAL CITIZENSHIP: Understanding nurtures responsible global citizenship by fostering awareness of our collective responsibility towards each other and the planet. By understanding the global consequences of our actions, we can make informed decisions that prioritize the well-being of all. This mindset of responsible global citizenship fuels advocacy, activism, and policy changes that contribute to a better world.

Understanding has the power to create a ripple effect of positive change with far-reaching global impact. By building bridges, nurturing empathy, challenging stereotypes, fostering effective communication, promoting peace, advancing global cooperation, inspiring individual actions, and encouraging responsible global citizenship, we can collectively work towards a more interconnected, equitable, and sustainable world. Each act of understanding contributes to the larger ripple effect, creating a better future for generations to come.

UNLEASHING THE POWER OF UNDERSTANDING TO ADDRESS GLOBAL CHALLENGES

Unleashing the power of understanding is crucial for addressing the complex global challenges we face today. By cultivating a deep and comprehensive understanding of these challenges, as well as the diverse perspectives and interconnectedness of our world, we can pave the way for effective solutions and positive change. Here's how understanding can be harnessed to address global challenges:

COMPREHENSIVE PROBLEM ANALYSIS: Understanding begins with a thorough analysis of global challenges. By seeking a multifaceted understanding of the root causes, impacts, and dynamics of complex issues such as climate change, poverty, inequality, and conflict, we can develop targeted and sustainable solutions. This understanding involves considering social, economic, political, and environmental factors, as well as the diverse perspectives of affected communities.

INTERDISCIPLINARY COLLABORATION: Addressing global challenges requires collaboration across disciplines and sectors. Understanding fosters collaboration by enabling individuals from different fields to come together, share knowledge, and leverage their expertise to develop holistic and innovative solutions. By recognizing the value of diverse perspectives, we can create synergistic partnerships that enhance the effectiveness of our efforts.

CULTIVATING EMPATHY AND GLOBAL SOLIDARITY: Understanding promotes empathy and a sense of global solidarity. By deepening our understanding of the experiences and struggles of individuals and communities affected by global challenges, we can develop a sense of shared responsibility and a commitment to collective action. This empathy fuels advocacy, support, and efforts to alleviate suffering and promote justice on a global scale.

PROMOTING CROSS-CULTURAL DIALOGUE: Understanding is enhanced through cross-cultural dialogue. By engaging in open and respectful conversations with individuals from different cultural backgrounds, we can foster mutual understanding and bridge divides. Such dialogue facilitates the exchange of ideas, knowledge, and best practices, leading to innovative solutions that integrate diverse perspectives.

ADVOCACY AND RAISING AWARENESS: Understanding empowers individuals to become advocates for change. By deepening our understanding of global challenges, we can raise awareness, engage in public discourse, and advocate for policy changes and initiatives that address these challenges. Through education, media engagement, and grassroots activism, we can mobilize collective action and drive transformative change.

SUPPORTING SUSTAINABLE DEVELOPMENT: Understanding is essential for sustainable development efforts. By comprehending the interconnectedness of social, economic, and environmental factors, we can implement development practices that are inclusive, environmentally friendly, and economically viable. This understanding enables us to design and implement sustainable solutions that address global challenges while ensuring long-term social and ecological well-being.

STRENGTHENING INTERNATIONAL COOPERATION: Understanding fosters international cooperation by promoting mutual respect, trust, and collaboration among nations. By understanding and appreciating the diverse histories, cultures, and aspirations of different countries, we can build partnerships that transcend geopolitical boundaries. This collaboration enables the sharing of resources, expertise, and knowledge, leading to collective efforts to address global challenges.

EMBRACING INNOVATIVE TECHNOLOGIES AND RESEARCH: Understanding drives the adoption of innovative technologies and research to tackle global challenges. By staying informed about advancements in various fields, we can leverage technological solutions, scientific research, and data-driven approaches to address pressing issues. This understanding ensures that our efforts are informed, evidence-based, and responsive to emerging global challenges.

Unleashing the power of understanding is crucial for addressing global challenges effectively. By fostering comprehensive problem analysis, interdisciplinary collaboration, empathy, cross-cultural dialogue, advocacy, sustainable development, international cooperation, and embracing innovation, we can generate solutions that lead to positive and sustainable global change. With understanding as our guiding principle, we can build a more equitable, resilient, and harmonious world for current and future generations.

COLLABORATING ACROSS BORDERS AND CULTURES TO EFFECT POSITIVE CHANGE

Collaborating across borders and cultures is a powerful approach to effect positive change in an interconnected world. By transcending geographic and cultural boundaries, individuals and communities can come together to address common challenges, leverage diverse perspectives, and foster meaningful and sustainable solutions. Here's how collaborating across borders and cultures can create positive change:

LEVERAGING DIVERSE PERSPECTIVES: Collaborating across borders and cultures allows for a rich exchange of diverse perspectives. Each culture brings unique experiences, knowledge, and approaches to problem-solving. By embracing this diversity, we can gain a more comprehensive understanding of complex issues and generate innovative solutions that consider a range of viewpoints.

BREAKING DOWN STEREOTYPES AND PREJUDICES: Collaborative efforts across borders and cultures challenge stereotypes and prejudices. When people from different backgrounds work together towards a common goal, they often find that shared values and aspirations far outweigh perceived differences. This collaboration fosters mutual understanding, empathy, and respect, breaking down barriers that hinder progress.

BRIDGING DIVIDES AND FOSTERING UNITY: Collaboration across borders and cultures fosters unity and bridges divides that may exist between communities. When individuals work together towards a common cause, they build connections, foster dialogue, and create platforms for meaningful interactions. This collaboration builds trust, strengthens relationships, and fosters a sense of shared purpose and humanity.

FACILITATING KNOWLEDGE SHARING AND LEARNING: Collaborating across borders and cultures promotes knowledge sharing and mutual learning. Each community brings unique expertise and insights shaped by their cultural context. By collaborating, we can share best practices, exchange ideas, and learn from one another's successes and challenges. This cross-pollination of knowledge leads to collective growth and increased effectiveness in addressing shared issues.

POOLING RESOURCES AND EXPERTISE: Collaborative efforts across borders and cultures allow for the pooling of resources and expertise. Different regions and communities may possess distinct strengths, whether in technology, innovation, natural resources, or cultural heritage. By collaborating, we can leverage these assets to address complex challenges more effectively and efficiently, maximizing the impact of our collective efforts.

ADVOCATING FOR SYSTEMIC CHANGE: Collaborating across borders and cultures enables collective advocacy for systemic change. By joining forces, communities can amplify their voices and exert pressure on governments, international bodies, and institutions to enact policies and initiatives that promote positive change. This collaborative advocacy can address global issues such as climate change, human rights, poverty, and inequality, effecting transformative change at various levels.

PROMOTING CULTURAL EXCHANGE AND UNDERSTANDING: Collaboration across borders and cultures facilitates cultural exchange and understanding. When individuals from different backgrounds work together, they gain firsthand exposure to different cultures, traditions, and ways of life. This promotes empathy, respect, and appreciation for diverse perspectives and fosters a deeper understanding of the interconnectedness of our global society.

CREATING SUSTAINABLE NETWORKS AND PARTNERSHIPS: Collaborating across borders and cultures allows for the creation of sustainable networks and partnerships. By establishing long-term relationships and platforms for ongoing collaboration, communities can work together to address current and future challenges. These networks and partnerships foster ongoing dialogue, knowledge exchange, and joint initiatives, ensuring that positive change continues to evolve and grow.

Collaborating across borders and cultures is a transformative approach to effect positive change. By leveraging diverse perspectives, breaking down stereotypes, fostering unity, sharing knowledge, pooling resources, advocating for systemic change, promoting cultural exchange, and creating sustainable networks and partnerships, we can address global challenges with greater effectiveness and create a more inclusive, equitable, and harmonious world. Embracing collaboration and cultural exchange is essential for navigating the complexities of our interconnected world and shaping a better future for all.

AMPLIFYING THE VOICES OF MARGINALIZED COMMUNITIES THROUGH EMPATHIC ACTION

Amplifying the voices of marginalized communities through empathic action is a powerful and necessary step towards social justice and equality. Marginalized communities often face systemic barriers that limit their access to resources, representation, and opportunities to be heard. By actively listening, empathizing, and taking action to amplify their voices, we can help bridge the gap and create a more inclusive and equitable society. Here's how we can amplify the voices of marginalized communities through empathic action:

ACTIVE LISTENING AND VALIDATION: Empathic action begins with active listening and validation of the experiences and perspectives of marginalized communities. By creating safe and inclusive spaces for individuals to share their stories, concerns, and aspirations, we acknowledge their lived experiences and validate their voices. This helps build trust and ensures that their narratives are heard and respected.

EDUCATING ONESELF: To truly amplify marginalized voices, it is essential to educate ourselves about the systemic issues and historical context that contribute to their marginalization. This education helps us better understand the challenges faced by marginalized communities and allows us to engage in informed and meaningful conversations. By continuously learning and unlearning, we can advocate more effectively for their rights and dignity.

SHARING PLATFORMS AND RESOURCES: Empathic action involves actively sharing platforms, resources, and opportunities with marginalized communities. This may include providing platforms for their stories to be shared, amplifying their voices through social media, or supporting their artistic and cultural expressions. By actively seeking to uplift and promote their work, we contribute to creating a more inclusive narrative that reflects the diversity of our society.

COLLABORATING AND CO-CREATING: Empathic action goes beyond passive support. It involves collaborating and co-creating with marginalized communities, ensuring that they are active participants in decision-making processes that affect their lives. By valuing their expertise and involving them in shaping policies, programs, and initiatives, we empower them to have a direct impact and bring about positive change.

ALLYSHIP AND SOLIDARITY: Empathic action entails being an ally and standing in solidarity with marginalized communities. This means actively supporting their causes, advocating for their rights, and using our privilege and influence to amplify their voices. By recognizing our own position of privilege and leveraging it to create space and uplift marginalized voices, we can work towards dismantling systems of oppression.

ADVOCACY AND RAISING AWARENESS: Empathic action includes advocacy and raising awareness about the issues faced by marginalized communities. By using our platforms, networks, and resources, we can shed light on their struggles, challenge stereotypes and misconceptions, and rally support for their rights and well-being. Advocacy efforts can involve lobbying for policy changes, engaging in public discourse, and partnering with organizations that work towards social justice.

ENGAGING IN SYSTEMIC CHANGE: Empathic action extends beyond individual acts of support. It involves addressing the root causes of marginalization through systemic change. By advocating for equitable policies, challenging discriminatory practices, and supporting initiatives that promote inclusivity, we contribute to a society that uplifts and empowers marginalized communities.

CONTINUOUS LEARNING AND REFLECTION: Empathic action is an ongoing process that requires continuous learning and reflection. It involves examining our own biases, privileges, and blind spots, and actively working to unlearn harmful beliefs and behaviors. By reflecting on our actions and engaging in self-improvement, we can become more effective allies and agents of change.

Amplifying the voices of marginalized communities through empathic action is crucial for creating a more equitable and inclusive society. By actively listening, educating ourselves, sharing platforms, collaborating, being allies, advocating, engaging in systemic change, and continuously learning and reflecting, we can contribute to uplifting and empowering marginalized voices. Through empathic action, we work towards dismantling systemic barriers and creating a world where all individuals are heard, respected, and afforded equal opportunities to thrive.

CONCLUSION

EMBRACE THE JOURNEY OF UNDERSTANDING

Embracing the journey of understanding is a transformative endeavor that enriches our lives and promotes harmony in an interconnected world. It is a commitment to deepening our knowledge, challenging our biases, and fostering empathy and respect for others. Through understanding, we bridge divides, dismantle stereotypes, and cultivate meaningful connections that transcend cultural, social, and geographical boundaries.

By embarking on this journey, we open ourselves up to new perspectives and experiences. We become active participants in the diverse tapestry of humanity, recognizing the inherent worth and dignity of every individual. Understanding allows us to appreciate the complexities of the human experience, embracing the richness of diverse cultures, and celebrating the differences that make us unique.

This journey of understanding is not without its challenges. It requires humility, patience, and a willingness to learn and grow. It calls for open dialogue, active listening, and a genuine curiosity about the world around us. It necessitates acknowledging the historical injustices that have shaped our societies and working towards a more equitable future.

As we embrace the journey of understanding, we become agents of change, catalysts for a more compassionate and inclusive world. By applying our understanding, we can advocate for social justice, challenge systemic inequalities, and contribute to positive transformation. We amplify the voices of marginalized communities, promote empathy and solidarity, and strive to create a more equitable and sustainable future.

The journey of understanding is a lifelong pursuit. It requires continuous learning, self-reflection, and an openness to unlearn and relearn. It is not a destination but an ongoing process that shapes our thoughts, actions, and interactions with others. As we travel this path, we not only enrich our own lives but also inspire and uplift those around us.

Let us embrace the journey of understanding with compassion, curiosity, and a commitment to creating a world that values diversity, fosters empathy, and promotes inclusivity. Together, we can build bridges, break down barriers, and create a future where understanding is the foundation for a harmonious and thriving global community.

SUMMARIZING THE TRANSFORMATIVE POWER OF UNDERSTANDING

Understanding holds transformative power, as it allows us to transcend boundaries, challenge biases, and foster empathy and respect. By embracing the journey of understanding, we gain new perspectives, break down barriers, and cultivate meaningful connections. Understanding promotes inclusivity, dismantles stereotypes, and amplifies marginalized voices. It drives collaboration, fosters social justice, and inspires positive change. Through continuous learning and self-reflection, understanding becomes a lifelong commitment, shaping our thoughts and actions. Ultimately, understanding creates a more compassionate, inclusive, and harmonious world, where diversity is celebrated, and every individual is valued.

EMPOWERING READERS TO EMBARK ON THEIR OWN PATH OF UNDERSTANDING AND TRANSFORMATION

By embracing the transformative power of understanding, we empower readers to embark on their own path of personal growth and societal transformation. Here are key ways to encourage and support readers in this journey:

EMPHASIZE THE VALUE OF CURIOSITY: Encourage readers to approach the world with a curious mindset, seeking to learn and explore diverse perspectives. Nurture their innate curiosity and inspire them to ask questions, challenge assumptions, and seek deeper understanding.

Promote self-reflection: Encourage readers to reflect on their own biases, beliefs, and privileges. Encourage them to critically examine their thoughts and actions, fostering introspection and a willingness to unlearn and relearn. Self-reflection is key to personal growth and cultivating a more inclusive worldview.

PROVIDE DIVERSE AND INCLUSIVE RESOURCES: Offer a range of resources, such as books, articles, documentaries, and online platforms that expose readers to diverse voices, cultures, and experiences. By providing access to inclusive and diverse content, readers can expand their understanding and challenge their perspectives.

Foster empathy and active listening: Highlight the importance of empathy and active listening in building understanding. Encourage readers to put themselves in others' shoes, actively listen to diverse stories and experiences, and seek to understand rather than judge. Empathy allows for deeper connections and promotes compassion and understanding.

PROMOTE MEANINGFUL DIALOGUE AND CONNECTION: Encourage readers to engage in meaningful dialogue with individuals from different backgrounds and perspectives. Foster spaces where respectful and open discussions can take place, allowing for the exchange of ideas and the growth of understanding through shared experiences.

CELEBRATE GROWTH AND PROGRESS: Acknowledge and celebrate the steps taken by readers in their journey of understanding. Recognize that transformation is a process, and every effort towards greater understanding matters. Encourage readers to celebrate their own growth and inspire others through their own experiences and actions.

INSPIRE ACTION FOR SOCIAL CHANGE: Empower readers to translate their understanding into meaningful action. Encourage them to advocate for social justice, challenge systemic inequalities, and actively contribute to positive change in their communities. By taking action, readers can become catalysts for transformation on both personal and societal levels.

Ultimately, by empowering readers to embark on their own path of understanding and transformation, we can create a ripple effect of positive change that extends beyond individuals and impacts the broader society. Through knowledge, empathy, and action, readers have the power to shape a more inclusive, compassionate, and equitable world.

INSPIRING ACTION AND FOSTERING A COMMUNITY OF CHANGE-MAKERS DEDICATED TO UNLOCKING THE POWER OF UNDERSTANDING

Inspiring action and fostering a community of change-makers dedicated to unlocking the power of understanding is a powerful way to drive positive change on a larger scale. Here's how we can inspire action and create a community of individuals committed to harnessing the power of understanding:

LEAD BY EXAMPLE: Be a role model and exemplify the values of empathy, understanding, and inclusivity in your own actions. Demonstrate how understanding can drive positive change and inspire others to follow suit.

SHARE STORIES OF IMPACT: Highlight real-life stories of individuals or communities whose lives have been transformed through understanding. Showcase the positive outcomes that arise from embracing diverse perspectives and fostering empathy. These stories can inspire and motivate others to take action.

PROVIDE EDUCATIONAL RESOURCES: Offer educational resources, workshops, and training programs that focus on building understanding and empathy. Provide practical tools and strategies to help individuals develop their capacity for understanding and facilitate meaningful interactions with others.

FACILITATE DIALOGUE AND COLLABORATION: Create spaces for individuals to engage in open, respectful, and constructive dialogue. Foster a community where diverse perspectives are welcomed and encouraged, and where individuals can collaborate on projects that promote understanding and positive change.

PROMOTE GRASSROOTS INITIATIVES: Support and amplify grassroots initiatives that aim to bridge divides, foster empathy, and promote understanding within communities. Encourage individuals to start their own projects, events, or campaigns that promote dialogue, education, and inclusivity.

COLLABORATE WITH ORGANIZATIONS AND INFLUENCERS: Partner with like-minded organizations and influencers who are dedicated to promoting understanding and positive change. Collaborative efforts can amplify the reach and impact of initiatives, creating a collective force for transformation.

CELEBRATE AND RECOGNIZE CHANGEMAKERS: Highlight and celebrate individuals who have made significant contributions in fostering understanding and driving positive change. Recognize their efforts and share their stories as inspiration for others to follow in their footsteps.

FOSTER A SUPPORTIVE COMMUNITY: Create a supportive environment where individuals feel encouraged and empowered to share their ideas, experiences, and challenges. Provide opportunities for networking, mentorship, and collaboration within the community, fostering a sense of belonging and shared purpose.

ENGAGE IN ADVOCACY AND POLICY REFORM: Encourage community members to engage in advocacy efforts that promote policies and reforms aimed at creating a more inclusive and understanding society. Support initiatives that tackle systemic issues and promote social justice.

UTILIZE SOCIAL MEDIA AND DIGITAL PLATFORMS: Leverage the power of social media and digital platforms to reach a wider audience and share messages of understanding, empathy, and positive change. Encourage individuals to use these platforms to raise awareness, share resources, and inspire action.

By inspiring action and fostering a community of change-makers dedicated to unlocking the power of understanding, we can create a collective force that drives positive change at both individual and societal levels. Together, we can build a more inclusive, compassionate, and equitable world that embraces the transformative potential of understanding.

9 798852 080646